THEO: GROWING UP FAST

THEO: GROWING UP FAST

Theo Walcott

CORGI BOOKS

TRANSWORLD PUBLISHERS
61–63 Uxbridge Road, London W5 5SA
A Random House Group Company
www.transworldbooks.co.uk

THEO: GROWING UP FAST
A CORGI BOOK: 9780552160537

First published in Great Britain
in 2011 by Bantam Press
an imprint of Transworld Publishers
Corgi paperback edition published 2012

Picture credits: Pages 1–6, courtesy of Theo Walcott. All other photos
copyright Press Association Images, except debut v. Wolves, goal
v. Stoke and Champions League v. Liverpool, copyright Getty Images.

A CIP catalogue record for this book
is available from the British Library.

Addresses for Random House Group Ltd companies outside the UK
can be found at: www.randomhouse.co.uk
The Random House Group Ltd Reg. No. 954009

The Random House Group Limited supports The Forest Stewardship
Council (FSC®), the leading international forest-certification organization.
Our books carrying the FSC label are printed on FSC®-certified paper. FSC
is the only forest-certification scheme endorsed by the leading environmental
organizations, including Greenpeace. Our paper-procurement
policy can be found at www.randomhouse.co.uk/environment

Typeset in 11.5/16.5pt Sabon by Falcon Oast Graphic Art Ltd.
Printed and bound by CPI Group (UK) Ltd, Croydon CR0 4YY.

2 4 6 8 10 9 7 5 3 1

To everyone who has
helped me along the way

Acknowledgements

I would like to thank: my family – Mum, Dad, Ash and Hollie, Sebastian and Aurora; all my close friends who have always been there for me; the Slade family; all the coaches and scouts who have helped me, especially Malcolm Elias; everyone at Newbury and Southampton football clubs; all the managers, especially Arsène Wenger and Harry Redknapp; everyone within the England set-up who has helped and supported me; everyone in Compton Village; all my teachers, especially Mr Colin; Jules and Anne at The Lodge; David Beckham and Thierry Henry for the advice and inspiration; all my teammates past and present, especially Gareth and Jake; Warwick, Claudia and all at Key Sports; Caroline and Pippa at The Sports PR Company; Mark Hutchinson; the entire staff at Arsenal Football Club; Georges Prost and Andy Ritchie; Huw Jennings; Steve Wigley; Jonathan Harris and Transworld Publishers; Ollie Holt. A big thank-you to the fans for having the support and belief in me and finally a very special thank-you to Mel for always being there through the ups and downs.

One

They say seventeen-year-old boys only think about one thing. They're right. I had my mind fixed firmly on cars and passing my driving test on Monday, 8 May 2006, so I was at a driving theory test centre in suburban north London when my life changed.

I had put my mobile phone and a few belongings in a locker on the ground floor of Crown House in Southgate. Then I walked up a flight of stairs into a room full of computers where a group of people were about to sit their exams. It was packed in that room. We all sat at computers that had partitions between them so there was no chance of sneaking a peek at your neighbours' answers.

I was pretty confident. The practical side of the test had gone well. I'd had plenty of lessons over the previous few months, driving round St Albans. I'd train at Arsenal in the mornings and practise my three-point turns in the afternoons. I'd got the practical test out of the way. The theory was the last obstacle.

Some of the questions are common sense anyway. I remember one about what you should do if you are sitting in your car waiting for elderly people to get to the other side of a pelican crossing. One of the multiple choice answers was 'rev your engine to make them hurry'. It was tempting but I didn't tick that box.

It took about half an hour of staring at diagrams of no entry signs and people making hand signals and then it was over. I passed the test. I don't remember my score but it was better than 43 out of 50, which is what you need. Then I went back downstairs, opened up my locker and switched my phone back on.

It started going mad. There were all sorts of texts, some with long-distance numbers on them, some numbers I recognized and a lot I didn't. I didn't read any of them. I called my dad. He was in a state of high excitement. He was babbling really.

'You won't believe what's just happened,' he said.

'I passed my test, by the way,' I said.

'Don't worry about that,' Dad said. 'You're going to the World Cup.'

* * *

When I signed for Arsenal in January 2006, I never imagined even in my wildest dreams that I'd be going to the World Cup finals in Germany with England that summer. It was daunting enough just thinking about trying to hold my own in training at London Colney with players like Thierry Henry, Ashley Cole and Robert Pires. The height of my ambition at that point was to play a few games for Arsenal in the Premier League. Nothing more than that.

As the second half of that 2005–06 season wore on and I hadn't yet forced my way into Arsène Wenger's thinking, it didn't cross my mind that Sven-Göran Eriksson would be considering me, even at the margins of his options. Michael Owen had been out injured with a broken foot since the end of December but even though his recovery had taken longer than expected he was back in the Newcastle United team by the end of April. Emile Heskey was out of favour at that time but Peter Crouch was doing well at Liverpool, and there was Jermain Defoe, who was in his first spell at Spurs, Andy Johnson at Crystal Palace, and Darren Bent, who was banging in goals for Charlton Athletic. It wasn't as if England were short of fast wide men either. Aaron Lennon was in great form for Spurs and Shaun Wright-Phillips had played some brilliant games for Chelsea. Both of them were competing with England captain David Beckham for the places on the right of midfield.

Then there was Wayne Rooney. He had been one of the players of the tournament at the European Championship in Portugal in 2004. He was absolutely untouchable out there, extremely hard to mark and running fast and furiously at some of the best defenders in the world, who didn't seem to know how to handle him. He was an eighteen-year-old phenomenon back then. In fact, we would probably have won it if he hadn't been injured in the quarter-final against Portugal. He broke the fifth metatarsal bone in his right foot, which meant he had to be substituted. He would have missed the rest of the tournament even if England had beaten Portugal. But we didn't. I was a fan like everyone else at the time. I just wondered what might have been if he had stayed fit.

Rooney had a guaranteed place in the World Cup squad two years later, but then the metatarsal curse struck again. This time it was the fourth one in his right foot, which he broke at the end of April in a tackle with the Chelsea defender Paulo Ferreira during Manchester United's league match at Stamford Bridge. That made him a serious doubt, but England were desperate to get him fit, even if it meant they would be without him for their opening couple of games. They clearly felt that was a gamble worth taking. The situation was very similar to when Beckham had broken a metatarsal a couple of months before the 2002 World Cup in Japan and South Korea.

Rooney had burst on to the Premier League scene when he was even younger than me, but in many ways he was better equipped to make his mark. I was still growing into a man when I arrived at Arsenal but Wayne was already fully developed and as strong as a bull when he burst into Everton's first team. He could hold his own with Premier League defenders from the moment he made his debut for Everton.

I'd turned seventeen in March 2006. Arsenal were going well in the Champions League at the time and I was included in the squad for the first leg of the second-round tie against Real Madrid at the Bernabéu. But I didn't get off the bench and I didn't really get close to getting a chance in the Premier League that season.

I knew the World Cup was coming up and a couple of people had mentioned to me that they thought I might have an outside chance of being included in the initial thirty-man party. My dad started going mad with the speculation of it all but I just couldn't see it happening. I thought it would be ridiculous to put someone in the England squad who hadn't even played in the Premier League.

There was no precedent for it. Not really. Other players had played for England without playing in the top flight. Steve Bull had won England caps in the late eighties and early nineties when he was turning out in the lower divisions for Wolverhampton Wanderers, but he had established a record as a phenomenal goalscorer by then. He was untried at the top level but he had earned his call-ups with consistent scoring. That had all happened fifteen or so years ago, anyway. Football had moved on. I thought my chances of making the squad were minimal.

Then something happened that made me think all the speculation wasn't quite so unfounded. A couple of weeks before the final squad announcement was due, I was playing in a match in training at Colney, which is just inside the M25, pretty much due north of London. It wasn't even a match on a full-scale pitch. It was a short-sided game, the type that Arsène Wenger uses to try to put the emphasis on technique and control and fast passing, the type that hones Arsenal's beautiful football. Some time during the game I looked over towards the touchline and saw Mr Eriksson talking to Mr Wenger, who is universally known at Arsenal as 'the Boss'. I still didn't think much of it. I presumed the England manager was there to check on Sol Campbell and Ashley Cole.

Sol had clattered me a couple of times, which had been his habit since my first day of training, and I did quite well against Ashley but I didn't do anything spectacular. I was beginning to feel more confident in training against players of that calibre and I had the thing that young players have when they are first emerging: no fear.

When we got back to the changing rooms, Sol and Ashley started teasing me about how Mr Eriksson had been there to watch me. Gaël Clichy, who was Arsenal's reserve left-back then, wound me up a bit about it too. I thought they were all joking. But then the Boss called me into his office and told me that, actually, they were right: Mr Eriksson had been there to watch me and gauge my progress as he weighed up his options for the summer. I felt a bit scared.

The Boss was totally straight with me about it. He didn't joke or tease. He never gives out any signs. He just told me what Sven had said. There was no question of any club versus country conflict for him at that point. I imagine he felt that if Mr Eriksson did take me to Germany, it would be great experience for one of Arsenal's young players. I'd benefit from being in close proximity to the country's established inter-nationals. I had hardly been a regular in the Arsenal side so it wasn't as if I was going to come back from the World Cup exhausted if I made the squad.

I told my dad what had happened and it sent him into a bit of a spin. Actually, it sent him into a lot of a spin. But then, after that training session, everything went quiet again. I never saw Mr Eriksson at Colney again. I still hadn't even spoken to him when 8 May came round and he announced the names of the twenty-three men who would be travelling to Germany.

At least those few months training with the Arsenal first team gave me a bit of experience of playing with elite footballers. It was good just to be around big players, stars, players I used to watch on TV. Dennis Bergkamp was still at the club when I joined and I was able to watch him in training in his last six months as an Arsenal player. He was amazing. Just watching him was a great education for a young player like me. In fact, when I first joined Arsenal, training took me aback. It was such a good standard. It was so much quicker than what I had been used to before. At first, I wondered if I would be able to cope with it. But the other players reassured me and told me to play my normal game. When you start training with the first team, you just want to get the ball to the best players. You don't want to take any responsibility. You don't want to risk making a fool of yourself. But as the months went by I grew more confident and the other players grew more confident in me and began to trust me.

I didn't really feel part of Arsenal's run to the Champions League Final that season but there were aspects of travelling with the team that helped me. When we played Real Madrid at the Bernabéu, I met David Beckham for the first time in the tunnel. He came over, shook my hand and wished me all the best in my career.

So when my dad dropped me off for that theory exam in Southgate I was only vaguely aware that the announcement for the England squad for the World Cup was being made that day. Dad told me later that he had persuaded himself there was an outside chance of me making the reserve list of five or six players who would provide cover if any of the initial twenty-three dropped out. But I didn't think there was any chance of that.

Then I came out of the exam, switched my phone back on and spoke to Dad. I tried to take it all in. There were people all around me when he told me so I couldn't have whooped and hollered even if I'd wanted to. People would probably have thought it was rather an excessive reaction to passing the theory part of a driving test. But I was too shocked to do that anyway. Too shocked and too daunted. So I just left the test centre in a bit of a daze and wandered over to where Dad had been listening to the radio in his car outside a petrol station.

Dad and I had this kind of *Lassie* moment. He got out of his car and ran towards me with his arms outstretched and gave me a big hug. It was quite embarrassing actually.

I got in the car and we drove back to the flat where we had been living since I moved to Arsenal. It was on The Ridgeway in Enfield and it had belonged to Edu, Arsenal's Brazilian midfielder, who had moved on to Valencia. I was very quiet. I didn't say a word the whole journey. I felt very scared and intimidated. I didn't have any experience of the pressure of Premier League games every week, let alone the World Cup. I hadn't got a clue what to expect, except that I'd be spending a minimum of three weeks trying to hold my own with the best players in the country, and then maybe pitting myself against the best players in the world.

I'd played a handful of games for the Southampton first team. That was all. Until a few months earlier I'd been living in digs on the south coast, sharing a room with other scholars in the Southampton youth set-up, having a laugh with my mates, playing in youth-team matches in front of fifty or sixty people. I was a late developer, too. I'd only been interested in football for about six years. It all seemed fast, fast, fast.

I soon got to know that there was a degree of astonishment among the press and the public about my selection. Well, I shared it. Mr Eriksson had picked Rooney, Owen and Crouch as three of his four forwards. But he had left out Bent, he had left out Johnson, he had left out Wright-Phillips and he had left out Defoe. And in place of all these proven Premier League players he had picked me.

It was such a surprise choice that some people looked for other motives in the manager's decision to select me. In January 2006, Mr Eriksson had been duped by the 'fake sheikh' from the *News of the World* and had talked to him, hypothetically, about being interested in the Aston Villa job. He had entered into a long conversation which was reproduced in the paper. Sven had had to apologize to a couple of the England players he had mentioned. It was embarrassing for everybody and Mr Eriksson was furious that his privacy had been invaded and that he had been set up. After that, the FA decided they would part company with him after the World Cup.

Some said that the knowledge that he would no longer be England manager after the World Cup, no matter how well or how badly the team performed, made Mr Eriksson gung-ho when he was selecting his squad because he felt he had nothing to lose by taking a big gamble. They said he would never have picked me if he'd felt he had a chance of being in charge of the England team in the years after the tournament.

There was also a suggestion that because he had been forced out of the job against his will, maybe he wanted to leave some sort of legacy for the future, something that would make a point to the men who had discarded him, and that picking me was his chance to leave his mark in years to come and claim a slice of credit for future England successes.

His own logic, which he only talked about after the tournament, was based on damning the more established strikers available to him with faint praise. He suggested he knew that the other forwards who might have gone in place of me were not ready to challenge the best defences in the world so he might as well go with a kid who was an unknown quantity.

I was happy in a bewildered kind of way, but I was surprised, too. I had never kicked a ball in the Premier League, I'd never even been out of the country on my own. And Mr Eriksson had never seen me play in a proper match. Actually, he'd never seen me play in a proper *practice* match. Just an eleven-a-side on half a pitch. It all felt a bit unreal.

He'd never seen Rooney play for Everton either, apparently, when he first included him in a squad for a friendly against Australia in 2003. People accused Mr Eriksson of being a cautious manager over some things but he certainly knew how to take a risk when it came to blooding youngsters.

Somebody tried to calm my nerves about my inclusion later on by pointing out that Owen Hargreaves, who was also in the World Cup squad, had never kicked a ball in the Premier League either. That was absolutely true. But there was the small matter of him having played in a Champions League Final with Bayern Munich. He was an established regular in a top team in the Bundesliga, one of the best leagues in the world, and he was about to be courted by Manchester United. That kind of experience counted massively in his favour when it came to pedigree. So it wasn't a good comparison.

Dad and I got back to the flat and he went straight over to the television and switched it on. I told him to switch it off. I knew there would be a lot of stuff about the squad announcement and about this kid nobody had ever heard of and I didn't want to see it all. If I didn't see it, there was more of a chance I wouldn't have to cope with the enormity of it.

So Dad switched the telly off and we played a bit of World Cup Monopoly. I lost. I was the gold boot; I think Dad was the football. It was a good laugh but my mind was pinging around everywhere. Dad was like a little girl, giggling. My phone was still going mad but I didn't reply to anyone. I spoke to my girlfriend, Melanie Slade, and she was as excited and bewildered as me. But that was it.

I didn't turn the television back on. I went to bed early. Dad switched it on as soon as he heard my bedroom door close. The squad announcement was on the ten o'clock news and my inclusion in it was one of the main items. There was footage of Mr Eriksson at a press conference at the Café Royal on Regent Street. A lot of journalists were flabbergasted that he had picked me. Their questions were laced with astonishment.

They pointed out that Rooney was a gamble anyway because of the lingering doubts about whether he would recover in time from his broken foot. They said that Owen was still short of match fitness because he had been out injured for so long that season. They pointed out that he had also become worryingly injury-prone. They said it was madness that if England were taking only two fit strikers to the World Cup, one of them should be a seventeen-year-old boy who had never played in the top flight.

Mr Eriksson said he had only made up his mind to include me in the squad that morning. He tried to convince the media that he had not taken leave of his senses. 'I don't know if other managers will think I am crazy, but I don't think I am,' Mr Eriksson said. 'If you expect Theo to have the impact of Pelé at the

World Cup in 1958, we are absolutely talking about the wrong thing. I am excited about it, that's good, and I think Theo will be a happy man today.'

Other people mentioned Pelé too. James Lawton, the chief sports writer of the *Independent*, said the decision to pick me was irresponsible. He said it was foolish in the extreme to compare my selection with that of Pelé in 1958. He was totally scathing about the idea that I could make any real contribution to England's campaign in the tournament. 'No, let's not play around with words,' he wrote. 'The theory here is that Eriksson has committed a scarcely believable act of football illiteracy. He has broken the most fundamental rules of the game by investing so much in a boy who has not yet had one chance to show how he might cope in a real match with real pressures and against the quality and experience of players likely to be encountered in a World Cup. Comparisons with Pelé, or even Wayne Rooney when he galvanized the England team so brilliantly in his first game, have to be discounted with maximum contempt.'

I'm glad I didn't read that piece. I'm also glad I didn't watch the news that night. It wasn't that the television reports were negative. It was just that I knew they would be going big on the shock element of my inclusion. It would have freaked me out.

When I got to the training ground the next day,

Ashley Cole and Sol Campbell both said, 'Told you, mate.' All the English staff were very happy. Sven didn't call. I still hadn't actually spoken to him.

Two

The day after the squad announcement, Dad bought all the papers. I didn't look at them. Any of them. Good job. Apart from going to training, I didn't go out that day. In fact, I didn't go out for a few days. I just wanted to get away from everything. I stayed in, locked away, with the curtains drawn. We weren't besieged by photographers because no one knew where we lived. Arsenal had kept that quiet.

Arsenal looked after me well. They arranged for me to do an interview with a couple of journalists from the national papers that would be pooled for everyone. And I did a photo shoot where the photographers got me to hold up the flag of St George. That was pretty much it in terms of publicity.

The club and the FA protected me as best they could, but there were some occasions when they couldn't help me, when we had to look after ourselves. When the Premier League season ended, I went back to my family's home in Compton, near Newbury in Berkshire, and there I began to realize the scale of what was happening to me. The villagers had put flags up that said things like 'Come on Theo!' and there was a lot of excitement. A lot of people wanted my autograph, and one day I just sat at the dining-room table signing stuff. Before long, there was a queue snaking up our pathway and out of our garden gate. Mel got plenty of attention, too. The papers found out where she lived in Southampton and she was easy to track because she was at college. Quite a few photographers followed her around constantly. A couple even camped outside her house.

When I was in Compton, she came to see me and one of the paparazzi followed her there the whole way from Southampton. He parked outside our house and stayed in his car all night. It was like he was a sentry keeping watch. No one had got a picture of me and Mel together yet, and because no one had taken much interest in me before there were none on the files either. Suddenly I was the flavour of the month for the media, the whole Wags thing was in full flow, and I suppose there was a lot of money on offer for whoever got the first picture of me and my girlfriend together.

It freaked us all out a little bit because it was the first time we had been exposed to that kind of interest. We'd met at a shopping centre in Southampton less than a year before so we'd only been going out for a short time. We were both only seventeen and it all felt as if it should be happening to somebody else.

After one day behind closed doors, wondering what to do about the bloke outside, we decided we wanted to go for something to eat in Newbury. The photographer had spooked us a bit and we found his whole approach kind of aggressive, so we felt determined that he wasn't going to get the first picture of me and Mel together. It was a bit evil, I suppose.

Dad phoned a load of the villagers and got them to come down to the house. Mel and I got ready to go out, and just before we got into the car, the villagers surrounded the photographer's car and refused to budge. We shot off and our friends kept the guy there for at least ten minutes. He was furious. When they finally let him go, he drove round the village like a maniac looking for us, but we were long gone.

A week after the squad announcement, just after the end of the English season, I got my first taste of the England set-up when the World Cup party went on a five-day training camp to Vale do Lobo on the Algarve in Portugal. Arsenal were playing Barcelona in the Champions League Final in Paris in the middle of the trip but Mr Wenger decided he didn't need me so I flew off with the rest of the lads to the resort.

I had never stayed anywhere as glamorous as Vale do Lobo before. They might have been familiar surroundings for most of the squad – in fact, I think quite a few of them had homes on the Algarve – but not for me. It was all a bit of a culture shock. It also underlined the reality of the situation: I was part of the World Cup squad. I was on a sunshine break with people like Steven Gerrard, Frank Lampard and David Beckham. I spoke to Mr Eriksson for the first time, too. 'Relax and play with no fear,' he told me.

But I felt really low the first couple of days in Portugal. For one thing, I was with all these great players who were household names and I was wandering around feeling like a spare part. There wasn't even that bridge between me and the rest of the squad that Sol Campbell and Ashley Cole would have provided. They were with Arsenal in Paris.

Most of the rest of the lads knew each other well. They had all been part of the set-up at one time or another. They had come up through the ranks together. They had played against each other in the Premier League. They were established stars who knew what it took to succeed. I didn't have any of that history. And quite understandably, a lot of them didn't have a clue who I was.

Most of them had their partners with them, too, and some had brought their kids, so there was less mixing than there might otherwise have been. Being by myself just made the whole thing seem that bit more daunting. I wasn't totally innocent in these matters: I'd lived away from home when I was a young teenager with Southampton. But we were kids who were in the same boat in the scholars' quarters at The Lodge. This time I was way out of my comfort zone.

Everybody in the squad stayed in their own villas on the complex. For the first part of the trip, I shared one with Aaron Lennon. He and I got on well, partly because he was the closest in age to me. Nigel Reo-Coker was brilliant to me as well. I didn't know him before I got to Portugal but I think he realized that I was feeling a bit unsure of myself and a bit lonely so he looked out for me. He'd ring me up and ask if I wanted to join him and whoever he was with for lunch. Stuff like that. It might not seem important but I really appreciated it.

But the day after we arrived at Vale do Lobo it all got too much for me. I rang my agent, Warwick Horton, and broke down in tears.

'I don't think I can do this,' I said to him.

In those opening days of the Portugal trip, I felt like this was a *Boy's Own* adventure that had all got a bit out of hand. I was worried that I wouldn't be able to live up to people's expectations and that the other players in the squad would think I wasn't in their league. I thought maybe there might be hostility towards me because I had deprived someone else of a place in the squad. I felt out of my depth, on the training pitch and off it. I felt like I was a stranger among a group of people who were each other's friends. Maybe it sounds ungrateful that I felt so uncertain about everything when I'd been given this amazing chance that every kid dreams about, but I was still trying to come to terms with what had happened to me and I was desperate not to let the fans down.

I told Warwick all this, and about how much I was missing my family and Mel. We had a good chat and he arranged for Mel to take a bit of time out from studying at college to come out and join me the next day.

As I said, Nigel Reo-Coker was absolute class. He offered to give up his villa and share with Aaron so that Mel and I could have a villa together. I felt so grateful to him. He didn't need to do that but he did it anyway. I think he could sense that I was struggling a bit and he wanted to help. There was a spell a couple of years ago when he got some bad publicity for a transfer or something and I felt it was so unjust. People were criticizing him and making snap judgements about his character and I wished I could ring the papers and the television stations and tell all the reporters what a decent bloke he was.

Mel arrived the next day and everything began to improve. I didn't feel isolated any more. I began to feel that I was doing OK in training, too. The FA kept me away from the press out there so I didn't have any media stuff to deal with either.

I met David Beckham properly for the first time in Portugal. He invited me and Mel to his villa. It was a lot bigger than ours. When we walked in, Victoria was coming down the stairs with her hair down and wearing no make-up and she looked absolutely stunning. I know it sounds star-struck, but that is exactly what we were. I know David better now and I think of him as a friend and a fantastic footballer, but back then Mel and I were two kids who were awestruck in the presence of these two incredibly famous people.

They were both very kind to us. They did everything they could to make us feel at ease. David was the England captain and the kindness he showed me in Portugal was an important step in making me feel like I was being accepted. Victoria took Mel off to talk about girls' stuff. She gave her some of her jeans from her own label and some tops too. Mel loved them. Neither of us were used to that kind of stuff. I mean, they were very expensive jeans. It felt like a real treat.

David was very encouraging. He just told me to try to keep enjoying it. He warned me that there would always be some people who would try to have a go at me but that I'd get plenty of support too. One of the things that struck me about him was that even though he'd taken a lot of criticism for various things throughout his career, he wasn't bitter or defensive about the treatment he'd received from the media. He didn't slag off the press or suggest that I should try to avoid them. Nothing like that. He was just very relaxed, calm and positive about everything that was going to happen in the weeks ahead. He had been through situations a lot more daunting than what I was experiencing so he was proof that if you gritted your teeth, you could survive and prosper.

So I started to enjoy Portugal. I loved watching Michael Owen in training. His finishing was un-believable. He just made it look so easy. Steven Gerrard was a great trainer. John Terry's commitment was awesome. I got more and more confident as the trip wore on and I got to know the other lads and the coaching staff a bit. When the trip was over, I already felt I was reaping the rewards of being around players of that calibre.

The whirl of excitement and adrenalin continued when we got back to England. I was on the bench for an England B game against Belarus at the Madejski Stadium in Reading. It was a strange match. Hargreaves, who went on to be one of England's best performers in the World Cup, was booed by England fans who had convinced themselves he wasn't good enough. Mr Eriksson had played him in a few different positions so he had never really had a settled run in the side. It was obvious to everyone in the squad that he was a class player but he needed to have a run in the holding role in the centre of midfield where he had excelled with Bayern Munich. I felt sorry for him. I was embarrassed that our own fans would do that to someone they were supposed to be supporting.

And for many others, the game was memorable only for the fact that England lost 2–1 and that poor Rob Green damaged knee ligaments taking a goal kick. He was wearing the number 13. His left knee just crumpled underneath him and he had to be carried off on a stretcher in agony. That was the end of his World Cup. It was a cruel reminder of how a random injury can wreck someone's dreams. To add insult to his injury, one of the Belarus players controlled the ball as Rob lay on the floor screaming and booted it past him into the net for an equalizer.

But I loved the whole occasion. I was the local boy from nearby Newbury and I revelled in that. I started on the bench but I got on midway through the second half in place of Michael Owen. That felt strange, because my first memory of watching football is seeing Owen score against Argentina in the 1998 World Cup when he beat practically the entire opposition. He had been a prodigy himself once, but now he was a veteran and I was replacing him.

Michael had had a tough year. He had signed for Newcastle United at the start of the season but his campaign had been blighted by injuries. He'd broken his foot in a challenge with Tottenham's goalkeeper, Paul Robinson, in a league game at White Hart Lane on New Year's Eve 2005. His recovery hadn't gone well and he had to have another operation. The result was that he was still short of match fitness in the build-up to the World Cup.

I got a great round of applause when I came on and I drew a lot of confidence from the game. I had a half-volley from a long way out that went wide and I generally enjoyed myself. It felt great to get some action and to be playing. I had only been in the spotlight for a couple of weeks and already I felt like I needed the release of getting out on to the pitch where the game was all that mattered.

Five days later, I got another game. Not just any

game, though. Because on 30 May 2006, at Old Trafford, I became the youngest player ever to appear for England when I came off the bench, for Michael Owen again, in the friendly against Hungary. This wasn't a B game. This was the real thing. I was seventeen years and seventy-five days old when I replaced Michael after sixty-five minutes.

Rooney had set the previous record when he won his first cap in a friendly against Australia on 12 February 2003 at the ripe old age of seventeen years and 111 days. Owen was eighteen years and fifty-nine days when he made his debut. Duncan Edwards, the great Manchester United player killed in the Munich air disaster of 1958, was eighteen years and 184 days when he first pulled on an England shirt. It was quite a roll-call.

They say that youth is wasted on the young, and perhaps my England debut was a case in point. I'd love to be able to say that my head was filled with profound thoughts about the great players who had gone before me as I waited on that Old Trafford touchline, but it wasn't. I was just trying to think about the instructions Mr Eriksson had given me and concentrate on not making a fool of myself in front of more than fifty-six thousand fans. And I was thinking the obvious: that I was about to become an England player.

Being the youngest ever, beating Rooney, Owen and the rest, didn't mean anything to me. It meant a lot to Mum and Dad, though. They'd got used to me beating records as a kid. They were mainly connected with Southampton, though. This was in a different league. This was the daddy of them all. But all that mattered to me was that I was playing for England. That was the main thing. I wasn't thinking of the significance of what I was achieving.

I did OK during the game. I had a couple of runs which didn't come to much but I didn't let myself or the team down. We were 2–1 up when I came on and Peter Crouch scored a third towards the end to extend our margin of victory. When the final whistle went, I looked up into the stands as I was walking off and saw my family. I felt very proud as I walked over to the tunnel.

We had one more game before we left for Germany. Three days after the victory over Hungary, we thrashed Jamaica 6–0 at Old Trafford. Crouch got a hat-trick and did his robot-dance celebration, but he fluffed a penalty when he dinked it over the bar. Mr Eriksson used five substitutes but I wasn't one of them, and he left Crouch and Owen on for the entire ninety minutes. I didn't read anything into that, but maybe I should have done.

I was still trying to shield myself from the reaction

to my involvement in the squad. Warwick told me that it had been mixed but he stressed that most people had been positive. Again, I know now that some people were heavily critical of my inclusion. 'I almost fell over when I heard,' Steven Gerrard wrote in his autobiography about the moment when he was told I was in the squad. Paul Parker, the former England right-back, chose the aftermath of the Hungary game to make his feelings known. He repeated the argument that Mr Eriksson would never have picked me if he had not been leaving the job after the tournament. He said it was an insult to other players that I had been picked when I couldn't even get into my own club's first team. He said the manager couldn't possibly have been able to tell what kind of form I was in because he didn't have anything to judge me by.

I'm glad I didn't know what Parker was writing and what some members of the England squad were thinking because it would have destroyed me. I did of course know that many people had their doubts about my inclusion in the squad, but when I boarded the plane to Germany at the beginning of June I thought I'd just have to prove them wrong during the tournament.

Three

The plane that took us to Germany was called *Pride of the Nation*. We touched down in Baden-Baden, in the south of the country, near the border with France, just after five p.m. on Monday, 5 June. It was five days before our opening game against Paraguay and there was still uncertainty about whether Wayne Rooney would take part in the tournament. He was due to fly back to England on 7 June for a final assessment at a hospital near Manchester when they would decide whether he rejoined the squad or stayed at home.

Until that decision was taken, Jermain Defoe was going to remain with the squad. That must have been difficult for Jermain to deal with, but he never showed it. He was brilliant in training before and after we got to Germany. Again, I didn't know it at the time, but there were a lot of people, including Steven Gerrard, who were secretly wishing that Jermain was staying in Germany and I was the one sweating on whether Wayne would be fit or not.

Even though the doubts lingered about Wayne's foot and his fitness, and Michael Owen had been injured for the second half of the season, England were still second favourites to win the tournament, after Brazil. This was the World Cup when England's Golden Generation of players – Gerrard, Lampard, Beckham, Ferdinand, Terry, Cole – was supposed to be at its peak, and though there had been some uneven results in qualifying, including an away defeat to Northern Ireland, there was still an incredible amount of optimism about our prospects among the public back at home and the tens of thousands of supporters who had travelled out to Germany.

I suppose that kind of heightened expectation is inevitable. There's no point in complaining about it because as a player you have the same expectations. This was a whole new world to me but I was still aware of an unspoken belief among the squad that we could do very well at the tournament. Other teams had a lot of admirers, particularly Argentina, but there was no side that was a hot favourite to win the World Cup. Carlos Tévez had not yet established himself as a superstar, though there was a lot of talk about what a great attacker he was going to be. People were also talking about how the African nations, particularly Ghana, were going to be stronger than ever before. Yes, Brazil were favourites, but not overwhelming favourites. So we went to Germany believing we could win the World Cup. That may have been a little bit too optimistic but it wasn't arrogant. Unless you go into a competition believing you can win it, you've got no chance.

And we knew we had the talent to make an impact. The vast majority of the squad played in the Premier League, which was by then regarded as the best, most competitive league in the world. And even if there were lots of foreign players in every team, being part of that league and playing alongside the best footballers in the game had spread confidence among our squad. I had already learned a lot from watching people like Thierry Henry and Dennis Bergkamp at Arsenal; the rest of the England squad would have had similar experiences with their teammates at other clubs. I know many people worry that the influx of foreign players into our league has restricted opportunities for English players to force their way into Premier League first teams, and that may be true. But I also know that I would not be the player I am today if I had not had the benefit of playing with and against some of the world's great foreign stars.

Our coach took us through Baden-Baden, a spa town where the players' wives and girlfriends would be staying, and then made the twenty-minute drive up to the mountain-top hotel that the FA and Mr Eriksson had selected as our base for the World Cup. The coach and its police outriders swept in through some grand gates that were the limit of the access for the media and the public and then down a long, sweeping drive with stone walls on each side.

At the end of the drive, the Schlosshotel Bühlerhöhe stood in splendid isolation. It was an imposing place, gazing out over the Black Forest for as far as the eye could see. And for a kid like me who was still battling homesickness, missing his family and worrying about whether he deserved his place in such a big adventure, it was a little forbidding, too. There was a giant stone eagle perched on the hotel roof, staring down at us as we got off the coach. It looked like a monster's lair.

When I got to my room, there was an action shot of me on the door. Someone at the FA had dug out a picture of me in an England kit from an Under-18s game. Nice touch. The room was great and I had a balcony with terrific views of the forest and the rolling hills. I could see Ashley Cole, Sol Campbell and Jermain Defoe on the hotel terrace, already in their shorts and soaking up a bit of sun.

I got all my clothes out and hung them up. I wasn't a typical teenager. When I was three, I was already arranging my shoes in pairs. And when my elder sister, Hollie, left home when I was in my early teens, I took over her room and cleaned it from top to bottom. She left it in such a state we didn't even know what colour the carpet was, but I soon spruced it up. I was an unusual little boy like that. So the first thing I did in my hotel room was lay out my toiletries neatly in the bathroom and put my boots and trainers in a straight line by the wall.

I went for a look around. It was a big hotel with more than ninety rooms but it was closed to the public for the duration of our stay in the tournament, so it was just the England squad and the coaching staff. We were scattered around the place so it all seemed quite echoey. I was on the same corridor as Aaron Lennon and Jermaine Jenas but it still felt pretty empty and quiet. It was a long walk to the meals room and the games room.

The environment intimidated me a bit, to be honest. At first, it just exacerbated my loneliness. Everyone else was a veteran compared to me. They had their routines all sorted. To begin with, they were sleeping most of the time. When I ventured out of my room, I hardly saw anyone around. The hotel was like a ghost ship. I wandered around the empty corridors and looked in the games room but there was nobody there. There's no point playing games on your own. It all felt totally alien. In those opening days on our mountain-top, I felt like I'd had enough. I wanted to go home and get back to playing for Arsenal.

But it got better bit by bit. Characters like Sammy Lee, the former Liverpool player who was one of the England coaches, make it their job to lift you. Training was hard in the heat but it was good to get out of the hotel, get on to a pitch and start playing. Every little thing I did well, Sammy Lee would point it out. If I scored a goal, he'd clap. That sort of thing sounds small and basic but we all need encouragement now and again. It's basic man-management, I suppose, realizing when somebody might be feeling uncertain and restoring their confidence. Steve McClaren was a good coach too. It all began to get my hopes up and made me forget about my loneliness.

I was knackered in training, though. The facilities were great, a superb pitch tucked away down a glorified dirt track in the middle of the forest. The pitch belonged to a small local club but the FA had upgraded the pitch and the training facilities. No wonder there were England flags draped over some of the houses on the way to the ground. But no amount of FA money could alter the fact that the heat was draining. It was great to be out there playing and getting booted around by Gary Neville, but the pace was tough. I am not a good long-distance runner – I am good at the short, sharp stuff – and I was taken aback by the endurance of the men around me. I wondered if that was what Premier League tempo was like. I thought I wouldn't be able to last it out.

At the beginning of most of the sessions, the media were allowed in to watch. There was a bewildering number of them and there was no hiding from them. It didn't bother me particularly but I would have had to be unusually thick-skinned not to realize that there was plenty of attention on me and that there was a continuing debate about whether I should be there. I felt that people were watching me in training to see how I was coping.

I couldn't help noticing how well Jermain Defoe was playing. Everybody else did, too. I was a bit in awe of the way he was training. He was the sharpest striker out there and he was performing as though he was playing for his place, or trying to force his way into the starting line-up. The reality was that it was too late for that. His only chance of staying with the squad was if Wayne didn't make it, and everyone knew in their hearts that Rooney was absolutely determined not to miss out.

At the start of the 2009–10 season, Jermain spoke about how the pain of those days and weeks after Mr Eriksson announced the squad was still with him. He said he would never forget what had happened, never forget the day when my name was read out instead of his. He remembered how the other lads would come up to him in Germany and compliment him on how fit and sharp he looked but at the back of his mind he was thinking, 'This is for nothing really because you've got to go home.'

The rest of the lads gave me a lot of encouragement. It was only later, some time after the tournament when Steven Gerrard's autobiography was published, that I found out other members of the squad had been dismayed by my inclusion and were watching me in Germany, thinking that I had no place there. Gerrard never said anything to my face. In fact, he was always friendly and bright with me. So when I heard about his comments, it was almost as if they hadn't come out of his mouth.

'Theo's potential was obvious in training,' Gerrard wrote, 'but as the 2006 World Cup dawned, he represented England's future, not the present. He had no right to be in Germany. None at all. I was gobsmacked to find him on the plane. Could Sven throw him into a World Cup game? No chance. Theo was still a baby. He was just not ready. I felt sorry for

Theo but more so for Jermain Defoe and Darren Bent. Jermain and Darren had worked hard all season to go to a World Cup and then a kid comes out of nowhere and takes the place they were after. It didn't look right.'

It might not have looked right, but it was the decision that had been made. To this day Gerrard has never said anything to me about what he wrote. I don't hold it against him. He wasn't criticizing my character, he was just expressing an opinion that I shouldn't have been there. And I can't really resent him for that because I agreed with him. I still agree with him.

On the Wednesday, Wayne flew back to Manchester, as planned, accompanied by the FA's executive director, David Davies, for a medical check-up on his foot. There was a lot of speculation that his boss at Manchester United, Sir Alex Ferguson, was fiercely opposed to him taking any part in the World Cup because he believed he simply would not be fit. But Mr Eriksson was equally determined that Wayne should return to Germany. There were reports that the two of them had a row about it, but ultimately there was nothing Sir Alex could do.

Wayne's visit was rolling news on Sky. It was mad. There were pictures of him going into the hospital, pictures of him coming out of the hospital. I was always convinced he was going to come back. In the first couple of days of training, even though the coaching staff were imploring him to take it easy, Wayne was kicking people as a means of seeing if his foot was getting better. Doctors probably wouldn't have recommended it, but it was one way of doing it, I suppose. And sure enough there were soon television pictures of him arriving at Manchester airport and boarding a plane for Germany. Later that night he arrived back at the team hotel, strode into the lobby and announced, 'The big man's back!'

It takes a bit of confidence to do that. A bit of bravado. Wazza is not an arrogant bloke. In fact, he's the opposite, but he's got a good sense of humour and he knows that the other lads like him and rate him. He was back, and Defoe went the other way, through the revolving door, on a plane home, his World Cup over before it had begun. Everyone felt bad for him, including me.

But it was a big relief to have Rooney confirmed in the squad. It was a real morale-booster. Just as Gerrard has said, Wazza's a one-off, a sublime player and a real presence. His skill is obvious. His reading of the game is brilliant. He's one of football's great talents. The other thing about him is that he always wants to win. Always. Whatever he's doing. A lot of professional sportsmen are like that. Ultra-competitive. But Wayne's off the scale.

In training, one of the common warm-up drills is this exercise called 'boxes'. You'll have seen it before matches. The players stand in circles of five or six, and one or two other players are left in the middle of the circle. Then the players in the circle start passing the ball to one another and the aim is to stop the lad in the middle from getting it. It's a kind of piggy-in-the-middle for professional footballers. In Germany, Wayne always played this like his life depended on it. During those first days of training, when he was supposed to be wrapped in cotton wool, he would fly into action when he was one of the guys stuck in the middle. He'd hurl himself into tackles to try to win the ball, and if he took someone out, more often than not he'd stand over them and yell at them to get up. I was looking at him and thinking, 'Bloody hell, that's what it takes.' Whenever I was in the same box as him and he was in the middle, I made sure I passed the ball straight away so he didn't get a chance to kick me. I got rid of it double quick, like it was a hot potato.

It didn't wind me up that he was throwing himself into the exercise like that. I admired him for it. He has just got that attitude. He wants to win no matter what he does. He's got a brilliant determination. He will do anything to win. You need people like him. His enthusiasm was infectious.

Rooney is someone who shines in training. Every player is scared of him. It's a combination of his physical presence, his determination and his ability. He gets on the pitch and he has already beaten his opponent because his opponent is so intimidated. He's the one player you don't want to play against. Even in training. You want to be on his team. At all costs, you want to be on his team.

It wasn't just on the pitch that Wayne threw himself into competition, either. A few days after we arrived in Germany, I walked past the snooker room in the hotel and Wayne was having a match with John Terry. They asked me if I wanted to join in and have a mini-tournament. I went in and watched their game. It was close, but when JT sank the winning pot, Wayne lost his rag. He got the cue and snapped it with his hands. He was so intense. It put the fear of God into me. I got out of there pretty quickly.

Once I'd settled in, there was plenty to do in the hotel actually. The FA had done a brilliant job installing stuff to try to alleviate the boredom that can be the enemy of any squad at a tournament between matches. The games room was like a full-blown arcade. There was a pinball table with a *Sopranos* theme, air hockey, table football, table tennis and a row of computer games. Oh, and there was a swimming pool, the snooker table and some tennis courts.

The more I felt at home, the more confident I became in training. I put myself about and tried to show the coaches what I could do. As our first game, against Paraguay in Frankfurt, got closer, we started to do a bit of formation stuff in training. I knew I wasn't going to be pushing for a place in the starting eleven but I was happy just to be feeling my way into the atmosphere of the group and soaking up as much information and advice as I could. I started to do better and better. It wasn't just Gary Neville who was kicking me in training now. I had a few battles with Rio Ferdinand too, and got his arm in my face when he brushed me off. Gradually, I was starting to feel like I belonged.

The closer the game got, the less we did. A couple of days before the match, I made a point for the first time of watching Beckham practising his free-kicks. I felt like I was watching a football god. His technique with the dead ball is just amazing.

And then the tournament was upon us. The waiting and the nervousness and the anticipation and the loneliness were over. Or at least, they all started to feel different. We flew up to Frankfurt the day before the game. *Only Fools and Horses* was on the television screens on the plane for the short journey up there. Once we landed, we went straight to the stadium to train.

Training felt great. It really did feel like I was a part of the World Cup now. I knew I was going to struggle to get on in the match the following day but the excitement was everywhere around the Waldstadion. Some massive television screens were suspended over the centre of the pitch, so low that Paul Robinson was using them for target practice when he was going through his goal-kick routine.

I could sense the nerves among the players, the way that everything had quickened and become more focused. Beckham went through his free-kicks again. Gerrard was a demon in training, even more than usual. Rooney was hurling himself about even though he knew he wasn't going to be playing – or probably because he knew he wasn't going to be playing.

There was security everywhere when we arrived at our hotel in Frankfurt that evening. It was swarming with people with walkie-talkies. There were hundreds of supporters outside too, and it occurred to me that a few months earlier I was turning up for first-team games at Southampton in a car driven by a mate and wandering through the crowds to the players' entrance.

It was also an interesting first full-on view of the media bubble we were going to be living in for the next few weeks. After we'd had our evening meal, I went back to my room and turned the television on to Sky News. They were showing footage of the England fans massed outside the hotel I was staying in. I went over to the window and looked down at the fans and the cameras and looked back at the telly to watch them watching me. I watched Poland v. Ecuador and then I went to sleep.

The next day was sweltering. I put so much sun-tan lotion on that I had a white face when I walked over to the bench to take my place among the rest of the substitutes. Mr Eriksson gave us a team talk before the game but it wasn't particularly rousing. That wasn't his style. It was calm and it was detailed. That was what we needed. I could feel the butterflies just sitting on the sidelines. The first game of a World Cup is a big moment in any player's career, whoever the opposition.

It was too hot for it to be much of a game. We got off to the best start imaginable when a Paraguay defender headed a Beckham free-kick into his own goal in the third minute. What a relief that was. But the rest of it was a bit of an anti-climax. Frank Lampard had a couple of decent efforts from distance but we had a few nervous moments when they were pressing for an equalizer.

I never really thought I was going to get on. I

didn't even get to warm up, which is usually the first sign that the manager is considering using you. I knew I would only get a chance either in some case of extreme adversity or if we were in a situation where the game didn't matter. And I knew that that was what my tournament was going to be about: supporting the lads and waiting to get a chance to prove to everybody that I wasn't such a mad selection after all.

The performance hadn't been great but the mood among the lads was buoyant when we got back on the coach. I had a video camera with me and I shot a bit of footage as we were pulling away from the stadium. Sol Campbell, who had been a non-playing substitute like me, was joking on film about how tired he was after doing his warm-down. 'I did some great runs,' he said. 'That twenty-five-second sprint was mind-blowing.'

We got a day off the next day and Mr Eriksson had already told us we would be allowed to go down off the mountain into Baden-Baden to see our families. Most of the players' parents and wives and girlfriends were staying at Brenner's Park, which was on the banks of a little river. That hotel became the centre of the phenomenon known as the Wags.

Mum and Dad were the only parents who weren't staying at Brenner's Park. They and Mel had booked into a small place round the corner called Der Kleine Prinz. It wasn't that they wanted to set themselves apart from the other parents, it was simply that they couldn't afford to stay at Brenner's. The people who were staying at Brenner's had signed up to an official trip organized by the FA and they were charging what to us was an awful lot of money. It was really expensive. I'd only just signed with Arsenal and I was seventeen so we weren't rolling in money. It was too much for us to pay. Anyway, Der Kleine Prinz was a lovely place. Dad got friendly with a few of the journalists who were staying there and who were all decent blokes who gave him and my family their privacy when they needed it. I suppose that, strictly speaking, Mel was a Wag too, but she was separated from the rest of the girls for whom Brenner's was most definitely headquarters.

Every time the wives and girlfriends who were staying at Brenner's went out of the hotel door, they were pursued down the street by packs of photographers. Even when they went out into the hotel garden to sunbathe, there were hordes of paparazzi perched on the other side of the river, snapping away at them. Mel and I didn't attract quite the same attention when we went out but we did get a few photographers following us wherever we went.

The whole Wags phenomenon has been so heavily

criticized since that World Cup that you'd think it was the players' wives who got knocked out by Portugal in the quarter-finals, not their husbands and boyfriends. I think the scale of the coverage was more to do with the fact that the news reporters working at the tournament for British newspapers didn't have stories about crowd trouble to cover. They had to find something else to fill their pages. Wags were the new hooligans.

I don't agree with the level of criticism that was aimed at the fact that the wives and girlfriends were in Baden-Baden en masse. But I do think that maybe we were allowed to see too much of them. I was delighted to see Mel and my family. I'd been dying to spend some time with them and it felt like a release for me to get out of the hotel. But the rest of the squad and I spent such a high percentage of our free time in Baden-Baden that it meant we saw a lot less of one another away from training and playing. That was bound to affect team spirit. It wasn't that the spirit was bad, but with a bit more time together it would have been even better.

The sense of detachment that I had, the sense of not quite belonging with the squad, meant that there were times when my time in Germany seemed like a family holiday. We had never been away that much together so we were all wide-eyed about how lovely

Baden-Baden was. We wandered around the narrow streets, took a ride in a pony and trap, swam in the pool, sauntered around the fountains. We looked like a normal family on a normal holiday. There were times when I felt just like a tourist.

I took a bit of footage of us all with the video camera one day. There's my brother, Ash, wearing his Armani shades and trying to look cool. There's me and Dad sipping Cokes in the Lounge Bar in the middle of Baden-Baden, watching Holland v. Serbia on the big screens outside. There's a busker singing 'Let It Be'. There are England fans bowing down to me as I walk past, and me looking in a jeweller's window at a keyring Mel had taken a shine to. A pap comes up and says there's a rumour I've hurt my leg. There's a commotion as a crowd gathers round a group of Wags as they wander down the street. It's like they're viewed as people from another planet. We play hide and seek with the paps who are following us. Someone mistakes my brother for Ashley Cole.

I had a few days in Baden-Baden like that. But we were into the tournament now and we soon buckled down to prepare for the next game, against Trinidad and Tobago. A couple of days before each game we tended to look at footage of our opponents. During our viewing of the Trinidadians, Mr Eriksson was as calm and as methodical as his public image suggested. He didn't say a lot in training but when it came to the day of the game and the pre-match team talk there was no doubt who was in charge.

The game against Trinidad and Tobago, the Soca Warriors who were supposed to be the whipping boys of the group, was in Nuremberg. The Franken Stadion is next to the ruins of the parade grounds where Adolf Hitler staged his huge Nazi rallies in the 1930s, but we didn't see any of that. It was the same routine: a flight in from Baden-Baden, a training session at the stadium – I scored three out of five in shooting practice against David James – and then back to the hotel.

We didn't play particularly well. In fact, when the score was 0–0 with seven minutes left it looked like it was going to be a major embarrassment. Mr Eriksson kept getting up off the bench with a worried expression on his face. That was the first time I had seen that. There was one moment when my heart leapt because I thought he was pointing at me to warm up. I was right on my toes, but then I realized he was pointing at Aaron Lennon, who was sitting next to me. So then I had to pretend I'd always known he wasn't pointing at me.

Aaron did particularly well when he came on and we sneaked a win. Peter Crouch scored a great header from a Beckham cross, then Steven Gerrard got a second in injury time, an absolute screamer. The England fans had spent a lot of the match chanting for Rooney, and they got their wish. He played the last half an hour when he came on for Owen. There was happiness in the dressing room afterwards, but mainly there was relief.

The result also meant that we had qualified for the last sixteen with a game to spare. The substitutes Mr Eriksson used against Trinidad were Lennon, Stewart Downing and Rooney, which meant that I was the only attacking player who was still unused. It was obvious that they were all ahead of me in the squad hierarchy, but I started hoping that if the circumstances were right – if, say, Mr Eriksson decided to rest some players – then the final group game against Sweden might be my chance to make a mark.

Four

I became more and more convinced that I was going to get my opportunity the closer we got to the game against the Swedes. I was doing well in training and my spirits were a lot higher than they had been. I was beating Jamo regularly in shooting practice, and after one session at our training camp in Baden-Baden, Steve McClaren, Mr Eriksson's number two, came up to me and said, 'Be ready for the game against Sweden because you might be involved.'

That sent my hopes soaring. If I'd been a bit older and a bit wiser, I would have known that it's the assistant's job to tell players what they want to hear. But it was what I wanted to believe so when we got on the plane for the flight north to Cologne I really thought this might be my shot at making an impact on the World Cup. The game was important in that a win or a draw would mean that we topped the group and avoided playing hosts Germany in the second round. But if Mr Eriksson was ever going to give me a go, surely it would be now.

We stayed at a Hilton in Cologne the night before the game. I had a chat with my friend the video recorder just before I went to bed. 'Hopefully, this is going to be my chance,' I told it. 'I'm really up for it.'

Usher was playing again on the team bus as it drove across the bridge over the river Rhine towards the Rhein-Energie Stadion in the suburbs of the city. The stadium was steep-sided and full of atmosphere. It felt like it was going to be a big night.

The game wasn't even a minute old when Michael Owen collected the ball near the touchline just in front of where we were sitting on the bench and tried to pass it. As he turned, his right knee buckled underneath him and he fell to the ground. He was clearly in a lot of pain. He crawled over to the edge of the pitch, signalling that he needed help. It was obvious immediately that it was a bad injury.

My heart was racing. I felt desperately sorry for Michael. He's always been one of my heroes, the person who sparked my interest in football when he scored his goal against Argentina in the 1998 World Cup. It was hard to see him like that, and I could also sense a fear among the staff that this might be the end of his tournament. There had been no one near him when he fell. It looked like ligament damage.

Then Mr Eriksson gestured at me to go out and warm up and my heart started racing even more. I didn't think of it at the time, but it would have seemed like fate if I'd come on for Michael. It was him I'd replaced to make my England debut a few weeks earlier, now an injury to him had created an opportunity for me to become the youngest player to appear for England at a World Cup. I wouldn't have beaten Norman Whiteside's record as the youngest player ever to appear in the finals, but I would have been close.

Mr Eriksson had sent Peter Crouch out to warm up as well. But not Aaron Lennon. I was encouraged by that. I thought my chances were better because Aaron had stayed on the bench. I had a feeling I was going to get on. We warmed up for what seemed like an eternity as Michael was being treated on the sideline. Then, when the stretcher came out for him, Mr Eriksson made his decision. He called Crouchie to the bench and told him he was going on.

I felt a crushing sense of anti-climax. That was the first time I began to think I wasn't going to play in the World Cup. I started to think it wasn't meant to be. If they weren't going to put me on then, when there was really no pressure on the fixture, it probably wasn't going to happen. It was the perfect opportunity. I wouldn't have had anything to lose. I was a totally unknown quantity. No one had a clue how I played. I thought if we were struggling, I might provide something different. But Crouchie was on now. There was nothing I could do.

We played well in the first half. In fact, it was the best we'd played in the tournament so far. Joe Cole scored a cracking goal, an absolute belter. He chested it down about thirty yards out and hit a dipping volley over the Sweden keeper into the top corner. Joe and Rooney and Lampard all had efforts that went close. It looked like it was going to be a comfortable win.

But we've got a bad record against Sweden, and when they equalized six minutes after half-time they seemed the more likely winners. Paul Robinson made a brilliant save to keep us level. There was no way Mr Eriksson was going to bring me on in that kind of situation, and when he took Rooney off with twenty minutes to go he went back on his decision to rest Gerrard. Gerrard cleared one Sweden shot off the line then scored at the other end, but Henrik Larsson got a second equalizer in injury time.

Back in England, my failure to get off the bench set off a new bout of questioning, about why Mr Eriksson had selected me for the squad in the first place. People pointed out that we were now desperately short of strikers and said it had been stupidity of the worst kind to include me in the squad instead of an experienced forward like Defoe or Bent. 'You lose Michael Owen against Sweden and take Rooney off because he was tiring,' Harry Redknapp said, 'and still you don't see Walcott. Why has he taken him? I don't think he will play now.' Others said much the same thing.

The draw meant we had finished top of Group B and that we would play Ecuador in the first knockout round, but it wasn't quite the morale-boosting win we had been hoping for. Sweden had made us look shaky for large parts of the second half and it was also confirmed that Owen had a serious knee injury and that his tournament was over. My own disappointment at not getting a game was insignificant against all that, but I couldn't help feeling frustrated that I hadn't got on. Not as frustrated as my dad, though. In fact, what he did next has made him a bit of a legend with some of the press boys who still laugh about it now.

Dad had travelled to the Sweden game on a bus laid on by the FA with all the other parents of the players. The routine was similar at every game. When the bus arrived at the stadium, it would be met by a FIFA official who would escort the families into the ground where they would sit together in the same area. If you think the fans get worked up about matches, you should see some of the players' parents. My dad's no different. He desperately wanted me to get on against Sweden, and like a lot of others he thought that the injury to Owen was the perfect opportunity for Mr Eriksson to see what I could do.

He was aware that he couldn't vent all his frustration at the ground because there was a bigger picture to look at and he knew that every parent thinks their son should be playing the lead role. But after the game, when the parents had gone back to the area where the bus was going to pick them up, he couldn't keep it bottled up any longer. He got chatting to the young chap who was standing next to him and started to let rip about Mr Eriksson. He was pretty candid about what he thought of the England manager, how he didn't have any bottle, how he was too cautious, how he had missed the chance to put his boy on and then England had been outplayed by Sweden.

It was all Proud Dad stuff. But it was colourful, too. There were quite a few swear words mixed in there, so this chap could be in no doubt whatsoever what Dad thought of the England boss. Dad kept going, too. He said Mr Eriksson's tactics were crap and he was beginning to think he didn't know what he was doing, and that if things didn't improve soon, we'd be out of the World Cup.

This bloke was very mild-mannered but in the end he turned to Dad and said, 'You shouldn't really say that.' Dad was a bit taken aback and told the bloke that he was entitled to an opinion because he was a football fan like everyone else.

He had just started on another tirade when he became aware of Jermaine Jenas's mum standing behind this bloke, trying to catch Dad's eye and drawing her finger across her throat. Dad kept talking and slagging Mr Eriksson off and Jermaine's mum kept shaking her head and drawing her finger across her throat to try to tell him to shut up.

After the conversation had finished, Jermaine's mum came over.

'Do you know who that was?' she asked my dad.

'No,' he said.

Jermaine's mum started laughing. 'It was Sven's son,' she said.

My dad was mortified, and he soon got his comeuppance. A couple of days later the FA staged a barbecue for the squad and their families at the Schlosshotel Bühlerhöhe. My sister, Hollie, has two children, Sebastian and Aurora, and she was pregnant with Aurora at the time of the tournament. She'd gone upstairs to my room to have a rest so my dad was looking after Sebastian, who was a baby then. Towards the end of the afternoon, the rest of us had gone inside but my dad was out on the hotel terrace, keeping Sebastian occupied, pulling faces at him, pointing out the scenery to him, that sort of thing. When he turned round to go back into the hotel, he walked straight into Mr Eriksson, his partner Nancy Dell'Olio, and Sven's son and his girlfriend.

There was no escape. My dad was like a rabbit in the headlights. But they exchanged a few pleasantries, talked about the weather and how well the tournament was going. Mr Eriksson said how well I was doing in training and was generally very complimentary. But there was a moment when Sven's son caught my dad's eye and stared at him with this slight smirk on his face. Dad said that in that moment he knew Sven's son had told his dad everything that had passed between them.

He was even more embarrassed now, so much so that he did the first thing he could think of that would get him out of there. He held Sebastian up in the air, sniffed his backside, said he had filled his nappy and he had to go and change it. Then he practically ran back into the hotel. I bet Mr Eriksson and his family had a good laugh about that when Dad had gone.

A couple of days later we beat Ecuador in the second round in Stuttgart. It was a hot, hot day and I burned on that bench at the Gottlieb-Daimler Stadion. David Beckham got the only goal of the game with a thirty-yard free-kick in the second half, and became the first England player to score at three World Cups. But I felt annoyed because another game had gone past without me getting on the pitch.

It was hardly a surprise, I suppose, but I was beginning to get really frustrated. However much I'd known it was a long shot that I would play a real part in the tournament, it was the worst kind of idleness to be watching, watching, watching when I was itching to get on. We weren't even training that much between games, which increased the tension in the squad. The desire to do anything to get out of the hotel grew and grew.

My dad was worried that I would be under tremendous pressure when I got back to English football if I didn't kick a ball in the World Cup. He was concerned that I would be ridiculed in the press. He thought, I guess, that once Mr Eriksson had selected me in the squad, it wouldn't have done any harm to give me fifteen minutes. I'm not comparing myself to Kaká in terms of ability, but when Brazil took him to the World Cup in 2002, he played twenty-five minutes in the tournament in a group game against

Costa Rica. It gave him a taste of the action, a feel for the tournament. I would have killed for twenty-five minutes.

My hopes were still high for our quarter-final against Portugal in Gelsenkirchen on 1 July, but once Rooney was sent off after a tangle with Ricardo Carvalho after an hour I knew I wasn't going to get on. We still gave it a real go at the AufSchalke Arena, despite being reduced to ten men for so long. Owen Hargreaves played like Superman. He was all over the pitch. His performance was a real inspiration. But we couldn't quite get the breakthrough we needed and the match went to extra time and then penalties.

It was a dramatic match even before the shoot-out. I think Rooney's sending-off owed a lot to the fact that he'd been playing on his own up front even though he wasn't fully match-fit and he had become increasingly frustrated at being so isolated and detached. There was a lot of controversy because the television cameras had spotted Cristiano Ronaldo winking at the Portugal bench as Rooney was shown the red card. That suggested there had been a deliberate Portuguese ploy to wind Wayne up and that they were celebrating because it had succeeded.

Steve McClaren had been shouting a lot to Wazza during the game telling him to calm down but it was hard to get the message across because it was so loud in the stadium. I didn't really see him stamp on Carvalho but I did see him lash out at a water bottle as he walked off. I saw Ronaldo's wink on television afterwards, too. You shouldn't be doing that to team-mates. I thought those two would never be able to play together at Manchester United again.

Anyway, Wayne was gone and Beckham was sub-stituted soon after half-time with what looked like a serious injury. He was in tears as he sat on the bench, watching the rest of the match unfold. Even if we got through, we knew we'd be without two of our most influential players for the rest of the tournament.

But one thing I learned is that the World Cup is about trying to get through to the next stage and then dealing with your injuries or suspensions as best you can. We'd already adapted to the loss of Michael Owen, and had we beaten Portugal we would have had to regroup and cope with the absences of Beckham and Rooney as well. Crouch would have been our only fit forward for a semi-final against France, so I presume Lennon would have started on the right. Maybe I would have been the first-choice substitute. Maybe I would have been the *only*-choice substitute. Maybe I would have played in a World Cup semi-final.

Maybe, maybe, maybe . . .

It didn't happen. The curse of the penalty shoot-out

struck again for England. I know it might sound crazy but I think we practised penalties too much out in Germany. We practised loads. I think we thought about it too much. It put pressure on us. Because of all our past failures no one has got the belief that we can actually win a shoot-out, and it gets to weigh on your shoulders. Lampard, Gerrard and Carragher all had their kicks saved, and when Ronaldo scored for Portugal to make it 3–1, it was all over.

I watched the penalties from the touchline. Afterwards, I put an arm round Rio Ferdinand to try to give him a bit of support. I wasn't a strong character so I didn't think it would mean that much coming from me, but it was better than nothing. It's poignant to think of that now, a seventeen-year-old kid who hadn't kicked a ball in anger trying to console the player who would lead England into the next World Cup. I didn't really know Rio. I'd hardly spoken to him. But like I said, it was better than nothing.

The dressing room afterwards was dead. It was like a deserted town in a Western movie with tumble-weeds blowing through it. There was just nothing. There was a bit of a commotion when JT and Rooney walked in. They were very wound up about Wazza's sending-off. JT was proper mad. They wanted to have words with Ronaldo. I stayed very quiet. I didn't want to say a word. I was just sitting in the corner thinking, 'Bloody hell.' I just wanted to have my shower and bugger off. I wasn't used to seeing people getting quite that angry. I didn't have the same kind of adrenalin going through me because I hadn't been out on the pitch. There were a few tears from the odd player, too. There were some, I suppose, who probably thought it was their last chance of winning the World Cup. I didn't know what to say to anyone. I didn't have a clue.

Gradually, people filed out of the dressing room. It was a really long walk back to the coach. I was one of the first on it and I could see everyone walking back, everyone looking down. Everyone had a Pot Noodle in his hand. Mr Capello stopped that, of course, but back then we were always given a Pot Noodle after the game.

The Portuguese coach was right next to ours and their players were bouncing around already. Ours was quiet. There were a few people whispering on their phones and a few people who were listening to their iPods so they could isolate themselves. I sat there alone, struggling to know what to think. I hadn't played a single minute so I didn't feel as much a part of things as everyone else. Wayne Bridge and Jermaine Jenas hadn't had a kick either so I guess they and David James and Scott Carson, the two unused goalkeepers, must have been wrestling with similar feelings, wondering if they'd ever get back to a World Cup, if they'd ever get a chance to play in the tournament. Those concerns became very real for all of us in the four years that followed.

We went back to Baden-Baden to pack up our things. I got a shirt signed by all the players as a memento. I got Mr Eriksson to sign it too. He apologized to me for not having played me but he said I did really well and that I had a great future ahead of me. I know he was just being polite but it was a small comfort to me at the time. I thought he could have given me a chance but I'm bound to think that. I can't change it now.

I think maybe if I had had a different kind of temperament, it might have damaged me mentally and affected my career. If I hadn't had the help of my family and Arsène Wenger at Arsenal, I might have been one of those players who is never heard of again. But luckily I had the right people around me. I'm the type who can let things wash over me to an extent. For the most part, I don't know what people are saying and writing because I don't want that kind of stuff to affect me. So I didn't feel it was a knock to my confidence when I didn't play at the World Cup. I was frustrated by it, but I didn't feel the negative attention that came my way had undermined me. I started the new season well for Arsenal. I played in the first game at The

Emirates and did well, and people were saying maybe I should have played at the World Cup after all.

But I don't think I should have been in the squad. I didn't deserve to be there. I shouldn't really have been in Germany. The following season a lot of interviewers told me I shouldn't have gone and I was thinking to myself, 'I know that, but you don't have to kill the kid.' Then there was Steven Gerrard's book, which upset my dad. But as I said, I agreed with some of what he said. Shaun Wright-Phillips should have gone instead of me. He deserved it. So, of course, did Jermain Defoe. They both deserved it more than me. But I didn't pick the squad. There was nothing I could do.

All I would say is that in the long term it helped me, and maybe it helped England too. When I scored my hat-trick in Croatia, maybe the seeds of that performance were sown when I was in Germany, watching David Beckham practising his free-kicks, learning from the work ethic of Wayne Rooney, seeing how Gerrard performed in training. Just having been there, just having been part of the squad, makes me feel as if I have been around for a long time. People expect things from me straight away. It helped me deal with those expectations. It didn't work out for me in Germany when I was just a kid, but I reaped the rewards over the next few years.

Five

My dad, Don, is a persistent sort of bloke. Which is just as well, really. Because he asked my mum out time and time again and she kept saying no. He was in the Royal Air Force then, at his first posting at Boscombe Down in Wiltshire, and my mum, Lynn, was an art student in Salisbury. She worked part-time at a petrol station in Amesbury, which was close to the base. Dad used to stop there to fill his car up . . . and ask her out.

He came close to giving up. He was told he was going to be sent to another base for a couple of weeks and then at the end of that he would be posted away. So he stopped at the garage for petrol with his car loaded up with all his belongings. He got all melodramatic and told my mum this was the last time she would ever see him. Except it turned out all his mates got new postings but he got posted straight back to Boscombe Down. When he got back, he asked Mum out again, and finally she agreed to go on a date. They were married in 1982.

I'm the youngest of three. My sister, Hollie, is five years older than me; my brother, Ashley, is two years older. We're all very close. I'm lucky like that. The five of us were a travelling band because as a young family we led a wandering kind of existence, just as my dad had done when he was a kid. His father was in the RAF too. He had come over to England from Jamaica just after the Second World War. My dad was born in 1958 while Grandad was stationed at Rinteln in what was then West Germany. They moved constantly: Germany, Cyprus, Lossiemouth in Scotland. Dad went to fifteen different schools when he was growing up.

I was born on 16 March 1989, in Stanmore, north London, where Dad was posted at the time. He didn't fly planes but he did plenty of almost everything else. He was in the payroll department at Stanmore, but when he was stationed in Germany he worked in a section called Mission Planning. Whenever we ask him about that now he gets all coy and says he can't discuss it. It's the Official Secrets Act and all that. Soon after I was born, Dad was posted to the Supreme Headquarters, Allied Powers

Europe (SHAPE), so the first three years of my life were spent in Belgium. I don't remember much about it. Just a big area of lovely woodlands near the quarters where we lived.

I had a very happy childhood. I'm the son of a mixed marriage but race has never played a part in my life. Maybe that's just a sign of the times, a sign of how much things have improved. Apart from one or two incidents, I was never aware of any comments or hostility. Why should there have been any, really? I mean, it was 1982 when Mum and Dad got married, not 1952.

Perhaps we were a little bit sheltered from anything that might have been said because we lived in a tight-knit RAF community for so long. But even when Dad left the RAF in 1996 and bought his first house in Compton, I never thought about myself in terms of black or white or mixed race. The only time I even glimpsed a hint of discrimination was when I was thirteen and a security guard at HMV in Newbury approached me and said I was acting suspiciously. Actually, he said I was looking 'a bit jumpy'. I wasn't. I was just browsing. The mate I was with, who was white, was doing exactly the same and the security guard didn't say a word to him. I was a bit annoyed about it at the time, but apart from that it has never, ever occurred to me that I have been the victim of racial prejudice. It has just never been an issue. It's not something I think about and it is not something I have ever come across at a football match, in terms of anything ever having been aimed at me.

Someone called me a 'nigger' in science in secondary school, and when I tried to hit him, the science teacher pulled me out of class as well. The kid was called Wayne, and we became mates after that. But that's the extent of the racial abuse I've suffered. I've never had any abuse at football matches. Never any monkey noises. Nothing like the England team got in Spain that time at the Bernabéu. And I am classed as a black footballer, even though I'm mixed race. Some people, like Stan Collymore, feel strongly about that. Barack Obama isn't black, he's mixed race. I know that, strictly, when people call me black it's the wrong terminology, but I don't really care. I don't dwell on it. I'm part of a generation that doesn't think as much about race.

I wasn't interested in football when I was a young kid. I wasn't interested in sport at all really. I kicked a ball around with my mates now and then. In fact, a nail went right through my foot once when I trod on a plank of wood while I was playing football. I went screaming home to Mum with the nail still embedded in my foot. Something similar, but worse, happened to Steven Gerrard when he was a kid, I think. There was never any danger of me losing my foot, as there was with him, but I did get a reasonable amount of sympathy.

I had an active enough early childhood, even without sport. When we moved back from Belgium, Dad was stationed at RAF Thatcham, near Newbury, and we lived at an old base called RAF Hermitage in a village called Curridge. Ashley and I used to go dashing around the countryside near Curridge, leaping from haystack to haystack up near an old path called the Ridgeway. I always pretended I was Spiderman, and I never tired of that game. I did get tired at school, though, apparently. Ash says one of his main memories of me from my first school, Curridge Primary, was how I used to fall asleep in morning assembly during the hymns.

The first time I played in an organized game of football of any kind was when I was seven. There was a charity match for a little boy called Peter Rowe, whose father lived on the base with us at RAF Hermitage, who had died of meningitis when he was two. Mum knew Peter's dad so she encouraged me to play in the game. I was a goalkeeper, probably because Ashley was the goalie for the other team. He saved a penalty.

But that was just a one-off. It didn't spark off anything inside me. As I've said, one of the things that got me hooked on football was the 1998 World Cup, and particularly Michael Owen's goal against Argentina. I was nine then, and Owen going on that lightning run and lashing the ball high into the top corner of the Argentina net made a big impression on me.

By then, Dad had left the RAF and we'd moved seven miles away to Compton on the other side of the M4. I'd started at the local primary school and made a friend called Adam Walker, who was mad on football. Every breaktime and lunchtime we'd do keepy-uppies and pretend we were making our own Nike advert. I thought about that when I watched the advert Nike made in 2009. Some of the footage of me in it was taken not long after Adam and I had been playing at being football stars. It felt like I'd been transported right back to those breaktimes.

A combination of the excitement of the World Cup and the fact that I had a mate who loved football got me more and more interested in the game. Ash was playing for a team called Thatcham Tornados, but I was ten by then, past the age when most boys have thrown themselves into football. Adam played for a local team called Steventon Boys, and I went to watch them occasionally. One afternoon I was standing on the sideline waiting for the match to start and they said that someone hadn't turned up. They asked me if I wanted a game.

I played, and I scored a hat-trick. It was a perfect hat-trick, too: a header, a left-foot shot and a right-foot shot. At the time I didn't even know what a hat-trick was. I can't explain how I did it. I'd never played in an outfield position in a match before but it just seemed to come naturally for me. I'll never forget that match because everything began to happen very quickly after that.

A decent local boys' side called AFC Newbury heard about how I'd played and invited me along to train with them. The following Sunday I played in a six-a-side training game and I could tell that the coach, Steve Taylor, was impressed. Put it this way: he told Dad after the game that I'd play professional football one day. Dad thought he was having a laugh. He told him he didn't even know I could play football.

I didn't know I could play either. But it was fun finding out. Scoring goals is pretty good for your enthusiasm.

AFC Newbury signed me up there and then and told me I'd play for them in the next game against Hungerford, who were their local rivals. Hungerford were confident because Newbury had just lost a kid called Charlie Austin who was a prolific goalscorer and went on to sign professional forms for Reading. (Charlie disappeared from the game for a while, but then in the 2009–10 season he started scoring goals for fun for Swindon Town and in January 2011 he secured a big money move to Burnley. He and I had played together for the district as well. He was a good player. I'm not surprised he made it.)

When we arrived at the match, Steve Taylor told the Hungerford people that he wasn't worried about the absence of Charlie Austin any more. 'We've got a little Brazilian now,' he said. That nickname stuck throughout my time at AFC Newbury.

I scored six goals on my debut for them. People just put balls over the top and I'd run on to them and whack the ball from distance.

Pretty soon, I started making plans. Back at school, my teacher got us to do an exercise where we imagined our future. I drew a timeline of the rest of my life with pictures of me as a professional footballer. I imagined I'd drive a nice car, have a nice house and win the World Cup with England. I'd have two wives – one would die and I'd get remarried (I haven't told Mel about that part yet) – and I'd die aged ninety.

I started keeping a record of my appearances for AFC Newbury in an exercise book. I drew a green and white AFC Newbury badge on the front cover and listed the games inside, with the result, how many goals I'd scored, what minute they were in, where we were in the table, pretty much everything. Dad caught the football bug too. He had an old video of him playing for the RAF, doing this one skill that he had – I call it the Don Walcott Special – and he made me watch that a lot.

Football got me into a bit of trouble, too. Once I'd got the bug, I wanted to play football everywhere. Including in the house. When I was inside, it was mainly keepy-uppy. One day I hit on a new ambition of trying to kick the ball to the top of the stairs, sprinting up to the top while it was still in the air and getting to it before it hit the carpet. But there were two problems with that. One was that I was never, ever going to get to the top of the stairs before the ball. The other was that Mum and Dad had these *Star Trek* plates hanging on the wall by the stairs. Oblivious to them, I tried to whack the ball up the stairs and it smashed all the plates off the wall. I knew they were going to find out so I told them straight away. And to my surprise, they were OK about it. They even managed to glue those plates back together. But they're not Trekkies any more.

I didn't necessarily need a ball to get in trouble. I used to get into a few scrapes with Ash now and again. There was one time when I was hurtling down the stairs, being pursued by him for some prank I'd played on him. My dog, Gypsy, used to chew plastic bottles and make them really sharp, and as Ash was chasing me, he picked up one of these bottles and chucked it at me as I fled. It was a perfect hit. It got me on the back of the head and sliced it open. There was blood everywhere. I had to go to hospital to get it patched up.

None of this interfered with the great days I was having at AFC Newbury. We won every game and every tournament we played in. It was properly run, too. The people who ran the club insisted on good parenting. Nobody was allowed to shout at the kids. Not that my parents would have been shouting at anyone. I think they were astonished that I kept scoring goals. Lots and lots of goals.

People said I had a fierce shot for my age. There was one time when I was at training for AFC Newbury at Thatcham and one of the other dads went in goal when we were messing about before it started. My dad warned him that I had a bit of a shot on me but the other guy just laughed it off. He obviously thought Dad was somebody who thought their kid was Superman. He saved the first shot I hit at him but the second broke his finger. You shouldn't laugh because the guy was in a lot of pain, but it was quite funny at the time.

I scored more than a hundred times that season and it wasn't long before scouts from district teams and league clubs were coming to watch me. Everything seemed to go right for me. We played in a prestigious annual tournament in Jersey that attracts a lot of scouts from Premier League clubs and we won it. I was the top goalscorer and I won Player of the Tournament. I found out later that Malcolm Elias, a scout from Southampton, was watching me and taking notes.

Swindon Town invited me to train at their School of Excellence but I didn't play that often for them. We took part in one tournament that turned into a farce. It was all supposed to be a big deal and we were told we had to arrive in suits. The club brought all our kit but somehow they managed to leave our boots in Swindon. So we had to play in our shiny shoes that we'd worn with our suits. Funnily enough, we didn't do very well.

It turned out that Chelsea had also been watching me at the Jersey tournament. It was where they'd spotted Graeme Le Saux a generation earlier, I think. A few weeks later I was invited to be a ballboy at Stamford Bridge for a game against Liverpool. I was incredibly excited because I supported Liverpool and I knew it meant I'd have a chance to meet my hero, Michael Owen. It might not quite have been the reaction Chelsea were hoping for, but I did my best to disguise my allegiances, even though I was desperately disappointed when Liverpool lost 2–0.

I had my picture taken with Owen, Robbie Fowler, Jamie Redknapp and, for the sake of appearances, Dennis Wise. We were shown around the dressing rooms, too, something I found terrifying. When we went into Chelsea's changing area, the first thing I saw was Gianfranco Zola's bare backside as he reached for his towel. I felt like a scared little pup because there were so many people in one room. It was fairly daunting. But I treasured that picture of me with Owen. I took it with me to the World Cup in Germany and showed it to him. It made him laugh.

That day at Stamford Bridge was Chelsea's pitch to me. It was hard to believe that a club like that was courting someone like me. I had only been playing football for a little over a year. It was incredibly flattering that a club of their size had identified me as someone they wanted to see rise through their academy system and into their first team.

Actually, I had a big decision to make. Because the Monday after Chelsea–Liverpool, I went to Southampton to listen to what they had to say. Malcolm Elias had been impressed with what he had seen of me in Jersey and he had also come to watch me play in a five-a-side tournament for Newbury that took place on some pitches by the town's ambulance station. Chelsea had tried to impress me with a matchday experience, sprinkling the stardust around, letting me meet the superstars, but Malcolm took a different approach. I had found the whole thing at Chelsea quite daunting, so it was a relief when Malcolm just showed me the academy side of things at Southampton. They didn't show me much of the first team and that made sense to me. I was barely eleven years old. I knew I wasn't going to be near the first team any time soon. So I liked their more down-to-earth style.

Malcolm, who was the club's recruitment officer, took me and Dad to The Dell, too. The ground was in its last years then. It was old and decrepit, falling to pieces. Malcolm showed us the boardroom with its trophy cabinets. It was nothing special. It was all going to be knocked down soon and the club was moving to the new stadium at St Mary's. But there was history in the place. It gave you a feel for the club.

After we'd been to The Dell, we were shown around the new training ground at Staplewood. We saw the academy set-up and a model of the new stadium – a vision of our future. Then they took me to a building called The Lodge, the digs where Southampton's apprentices – they called them scholars down there – lived after they had signed professional forms.

I liked what I saw. I liked the atmosphere down there. I liked the feel of the club. I was also aware that Southampton were willing to take me on straight away whereas Chelsea were insisting that I go to a trial first to see whether I made it into their academy system. Southampton usually insisted on that kind of process too, but they said that in my case they would waive it. I took that as a statement of their faith in me and the fact that they thought I was something special. I didn't get that feeling from Chelsea. There was more of a sense that I would just be another little fish in a big pond if I went there. I thought no one would ever hear of me again if I chose Chelsea. I thought I'd get swallowed up.

Dad drove us back home to Compton, but before we got there I told him I'd decided I didn't want to go to Chelsea. I wanted to go to Southampton. His mates at the pub said later that I must be crazy not to go to Chelsea with all the glamour and the famous names, but he let me decide. He told them it wasn't his choice, it was my choice, and we were both proved right.

That association, that choice I made, doesn't really add anything to Chelsea games for me when I line up against them for Arsenal. They're always big games and it's always a challenge to play against people like John Terry, who has incredible presence on the pitch and is always talking to the rest of his players, encouraging them, cajoling them, making sure they never lose concentration. There's not a lot of love lost between Arsenal and Chelsea these days, either. The clubs represent very different philosophies. Chelsea tend to buy experience rather than develop their own players. At Arsenal, Arsène Wenger stays loyal to his young players. Put it this way: I've never regretted the choice I made.

Six

And so a new life for me began. On Tuesdays and Thursdays every week, Dad drove me down the A34 to Southampton for training. He got off work early on those afternoons and fed me a plate of pasta as soon as I got in from school. Then we'd make the forty-five-minute journey south, although I never saw much of it. Without fail, I fell asleep about five minutes after we left home and dozed until we arrived at King Edward's School where the Southampton kids trained.

Training was good. The coach was Steve Baker, who used to be the Southampton right-back, and Mark Chamberlain was also on the staff. Chamberlain used to be a flying winger in his day too, a lad who was renowned for his speed when he made his debut for England in 1982 and scored against Luxembourg. His son Alex Oxlade-Chamberlain is pretty nippy too. Mark gave me a lot of encouragement.

Training lasted for a couple of hours. We did a lot of technical work. It was mostly skills and shooting. Everyone seemed very quick and skilful to me when I first started. It was a definite step up from anything I had been used to and I felt a bit intimidated. It took me a few weeks to get into the rhythm of it but gradually I got used to it. In one of my first matches for Southampton, I scored a hat-trick against Chelsea Under-13s in a 5–2 win. That was a real boost because it was an indication that I could thrive at that level. Another of the youth coaches, Andy Ritchie, recalled that game recently. 'It was unusual for us to score that many against Chelsea,' he said. 'Then my friend told me that this young lad called Theo Walcott had scored three. He hadn't even signed for us yet.'

Dad watched every one of the training sessions and all the matches, too. Never missed one. Occasionally, on the way back to Compton we'd stop for a McDonald's. We usually got back about nine p.m. and I'd fall straight into bed.

There were a lot of games in London and the Home Counties: Chelsea, Fulham, Millwall, West Ham, Reading, Arsenal. Many of the academy boys would get a coach from Southampton to away games, but Dad drove me there. There didn't seem a lot of point driving down to Southampton and then Dad following the coach back the same way we'd come. I loved those matches. I loved that time altogether. If anything got in the way it seemed like the end of the world. We turned up once to a game against Fulham in Cobham and there were no other cars in the car park. No one had told us that the game had been cancelled. I was so disappointed I started crying.

I'd moved to senior school by then and started at The Downs in Compton. It's a good school, well known for its academic excellence. I probably didn't do a lot for their average on that score but they were great with me there. They allowed me a lot of time off for football with Southampton as I got older. I think they recognized I had a talent and they wanted to allow me to use it. Maths was my best academic subject, but like most kids, I looked forward to breaktimes when we could play football. I took my studies seriously, but not as seriously as my football.

The only time I ever got into trouble at school revolved around football as well. Some kid ran off with our ball and when I tried to get it back he got me in a headlock. So I punched him in the mouth and he went to tell a teacher. I had to stand up against a wall for ten minutes as punishment. That was un-usual for me, though. I was always a mild-mannered boy. It took a lot to make me lose my temper. Just like it does now.

I was one of the only kids at the school who actually lived in Compton. The school dominates the community, though, and I loved my time there. You only realize how much fun school was when you've left. At the time you think you hate it, but when I left, I really missed it. It's being with your mates, chatting and having a laugh, not having as many responsibilities.

I played for the school now and then, although it could get a bit risky. I'd quickly developed a bit of a reputation because I was on Southampton's books and I'd scored all those goals for AFC Newbury. So I suppose some kids thought I was a bit of a scalp and a few of them came after me during games. I scored nine goals in a match for the school twice. We won the first one 13–2 and there was a kid on the other team who was basically trying to break my legs the whole match. In the end, our games teacher took me off to get me out of the firing line.

When Arsenal bought me from Southampton, some papers sent reporters to Compton and to The Downs to see what they could find out about me. I got off fairly lightly. My mates were actually nice about me. The guy from the *Guardian* spoke to my friend Tom Moore, who played with me at Newbury as well. The reporter remarked that Tom must be pretty good if he'd played on two teams with me. 'Not really,' Tom said. 'I just used to pass it to him and he'd run on to it and score. His pace and the power in his shot at that age were the things that made him special. We played a match on tour in Holland one year and he scored a triple hat-trick. We won 14–0. But when you play with a genius, it makes you more realistic about your own limitations.'

Gradually, I took more and more time off school. When I was thirteen, Mum started taking me to The Lodge on the Sunday evening and I stayed the night there and then trained all day Monday with the scholars before either Malcolm Elias or Mum brought me home (Dad worked all day on a Monday). The Lodge was run by Julia, Anne and Mike, who were great people. I liked the atmosphere of camaraderie between the lads there.

It was a great introduction to life as a young foot-baller. On that one night a week I had there, I just sat back and watched what was going on. There was plenty, believe me. There were a lot of jokes and japes, people coming back late and being ambushed by lads battering them with pillows, and then a variety of practical jokes that weren't quite as wholesome.

One night, things got particularly wild. Leon Best

and Dexter Blackstock, who both have good league careers now and were a few years older than me, had been chasing after the same girl. Leon was sure she was going to choose him; Dexter was equally certain she would plump for him. Except it turned out she already had a boyfriend, and this boyfriend belonged to a Southampton gang. There was a bit of tension between local kids and the lads who lived at The Lodge anyway. I think the locals resented us as outsiders who fancied ourselves because we were footballers. But this ramped it up to a new level.

The final confrontation happened on a Sunday night. We knew there was something afoot, and I was in one of the ground-floor rooms at The Lodge staring out of the windows at the front. I could see two lads walking towards Leon and Dexter, and then Leon and Dexter, full of bravado, starting to swagger towards them. It was like a Western showdown. Then I looked further down the road and about fifty people came round the corner, armed to the eyeballs with baseball bats, bricks, sticks and stones. Now it wasn't like a Western any more. It was like a scene out of that hooligan movie *Green Street*.

I was rooted to the spot, absolutely terrified. I was a schoolboy barely into my teens. This was totally outside my experience. Some of the lads were not quite so shy. I looked round and Nathan Dyer, who moved on to play for Swansea City, and Martin Cranie, who went on to play for Portsmouth in the Premier League and then Coventry City, were grabbing what they could to protect themselves and were heading for the door. They were all for going out there and getting stuck in. They wanted to back up their mates, basically.

But when Leon and Dexter saw the mob of gang members coming round that corner, they forgot their bravado and turned on their heels. The mob gave chase. I'd never realized Leon was so fast. I'd never seen him sprint like that in training before.

I had no idea what was going to happen but I thought I'd keep out of it. I went into the television room and sat down to watch something. I suppose I thought that if I turned the television up loud enough, all the fuss outside might just go away. But the next thing I knew a brick had come through the window and there was glass and debris all over the floor. All hell broke loose. Leon and Dexter had made it back inside but the gang was running amok outside, smashing cars in and throwing more bricks. It was only when Mike went out to remonstrate with them that they gave up and went away. Cameras were installed after that.

I was a reasonably good kid. Not much of a rebel, I'm afraid. My mate Jake Thomson and I did wind

Julia up once after we'd been to Reading on the train to get haircuts and do a bit of shopping. Julia was like a mum to us all and I rang her and told her there had been a system breakdown on the trains and that we wouldn't be back until after midnight. She was horrified. She started panicking because she was responsible for us and she was imagining all the things that might happen to us. Actually, we were right outside the front door. She was not happy.

Southampton was brilliant for me. I was very lucky that I got my grounding in football at a club that had such a good academy set-up. And I was particularly lucky to come under the wing of Georges Prost. Georges was a genius. He arrived at the academy from France when I was thirteen and he could hardly speak a word of English. But his coaching was superb. It was Georges who did all the technique work with me. It was Georges who helped to make me what I am today. He taught me to use both feet. He worked on that relentlessly. It would be fifteen minutes on the right foot, fifteen minutes on the left. He was in his early fifties and he had so much experience and so much knowledge. Everyone responded to him, and during the five years he was in charge of the youth set-up, Southampton had an incredible run of success.

He had come from Olympique Marseille, and

when he left Southampton, in 2007, after recovering from throat cancer, he took over the youth system at Lyon. Not many people in England have heard of him but he is well known in French football. When I mentioned him to Arsène Wenger and Mathieu Flamini when I arrived at Arsenal, they spoke of him very warmly. He still keeps in touch with my dad to check up on how I'm doing.

For me, playing youth-team football for Southampton meant a lot of goals and a lot of travelling. Dad drove me everywhere and we got through plenty of miles and a couple of cars as a result. We had one Peugeot 205 that did 189,000 miles before it finally expired. Once, we were on our way to Eastleigh, where we played our home games, for a match against Arsenal when our car broke down. I was distraught because I thought I was going to miss the game, but my grandad came out to rescue us. After the 2006 World Cup, I bought Dad a car to make up for all the ones that had blown up over the years.

People continued to try to make me a target, mainly because of my pace, I think. There was one youth-team game against Fulham where an opposition full-back called Billy spent the entire first half trying to kick me into touch. I know his name was Billy because his dad was standing on the touchline egging him on. 'Take him out, Billy!' he kept saying, every time I got the ball. 'Take him out, let him know you're there, hurt him, Billy!' The dad was relentless, and so was Billy. In the end the referee told the Fulham coach to take Billy off or he would be sent off. I could look after myself fine but it was a relief when he went off and his dad shut his mouth.

In my second year at Southampton, when I was thirteen, Dad bet me £100 that I couldn't score thirty goals in a season. That seemed like such a lot of money to me then. Well, it was a lot of money. When we got to the very last game, against Tottenham, I had scored twenty-eight goals. My dad was filming the game, and when I knocked in the twenty-ninth you can hear him on the footage groaning and moaning about the bet. In the last five minutes I won a penalty and took it myself. I hit the bar. Dad didn't know whether to laugh or cry.

The first time I started thinking seriously that football could be a career was when I played my first reserve match for Southampton, against Watford at St Mary's. I was fifteen, the youngest player who had ever appeared for Southampton reserves, and I played well. It had been a dramatic rise. I hadn't started playing football until I was ten and five years later I was in the reserves for a Premier League team.

Fairly soon, against a general background of bewilderment and surprise, it began to become evident that I had a chance of making a living as a professional footballer. Steve Baker and Mark Chamberlain had told my dad when I was only twelve that they thought I'd be a player one day. Mum said it was when I was thirteen that she realized I had a special talent. She called Dad 'Mr Negative' because he kept trying to dampen down the expectations. He was only doing that to protect me, but the Southampton coaches told Mum I was 'the full package'. They said my character would carry me through.

I'm still not entirely sure what they meant by that. I suppose I don't really let things get to me. I don't let people get to me either. I've got this belief in myself which means I don't let criticism affect me. And I don't get wound up by opponents. I'm not a particularly fiery person, I never have been, but I do have a calm determination.

My time at Southampton was a series of landmarks. I was playing in the Under-17s when I was thirteen. I made my debut in the FA Youth Cup when I was fourteen: I came on for the last few minutes of a game against Reading and skinned a few players. Gordon Strachan, who was the Southampton manager at the time, came along to watch. I was told he had been impressed. I was still fourteen when I scored the winning goal against Arsenal in an FA Youth Cup tie at St Mary's. That was a significant step forward for me. It was a big occasion. There were lots of high-profile people in the stands and I still felt comfortable enough to play my best. It was a good goal, too, a great first touch to control the ball before I outpaced the defence then finished with my weaker left foot. 'It was then that I knew Southampton couldn't keep him,' Andy Ritchie said recently.

It was around that time I met my agent, Warwick Horton, from Key Sports Management, who has been a major influence on my career and a good friend. I know there are a lot of stories about bad agents, corrupt agents, grasping agents, unscrupulous agents and greedy agents, and no doubt a lot of them are true. But there are some good ones out there too, and mine is one of them. I trust Warwick and Key Sports completely to do what is best for me.

Warwick bumped into my dad at an Under-16s international tournament in Montaigu, near Nantes, in France. I say 'bumped into', but I think Warwick might admit now he had gone out to France hoping to meet Dad after he'd seen me play for Southampton Under-17s against Aston Villa at Villa's Bodymoor Heath training ground. He'd been impressed with both me and Nathan Dyer.

Warwick introduced himself to Dad and they hit it off straight away. He came down to Compton to have a drink with Mum and Dad in the local pub, and that sealed it.

I needed Warwick's input fairly soon. In 2005 I played for England in an Under-17s tournament on the Algarve and caught the eye of a few teams. Arsenal, Liverpool, Manchester United, Spurs and Chelsea were all showing an interest and Warwick came down to Compton to discuss the situation with my parents. Mum and Dad left the decision to me. I told them I'd like to stay at Southampton for a little while longer. I liked the youth set-up there and I was happy hanging out with my mates at The Lodge.

In that 2004–05 season we went on a great run in the Youth Cup and got to the final. We played Ipswich and drew 2–2 in the first leg at St Mary's with goals from Leon Best and Dave McGoldrick. That gave Ipswich the advantage for the second leg at Portman Road but we had some great chances to win it. I set up a chance for Tim Sparv, a lad from Finland, but somehow the Ipswich keeper saved it from about two yards out. (I came across Tim again in the summer of 2009 when I played against him in the European Under-21 Championship in Sweden. We had a chat after the game. He said he remembered me being very tidy – and watching *EastEnders* a lot.)

We had other chances, too. Nathan Dyer had a golden opportunity to square the ball to me for a tap-in but he shot instead ... and missed. And then Teddy Sheringham's son, Charlie, who had been on the fringes of the Ipswich youth team, came on as a substitute and scored the only goal, the goal that won it for them. It should have been us lifting that cup. It was a harsh lesson in the need to put your chances away.

I didn't know it at the time, but the first leg of the final had already helped to shape my future. Arsène Wenger had come to watch the match and my performance impressed him. He said later Arsenal had sent scouts to watch me fifty times but that that was the occasion when he became convinced I could be an Arsenal player. 'The first quality that stood out was the timing of his runs,' the Boss said, 'when to go and when not to go. Sometimes you have players who are super quick but you don't see it in their game because they don't run at the right time, they don't use their asset.'

That FA Youth Cup Final was the high point of Southampton's season – the whole club, I mean, not just the youth team. It was all doom and gloom everywhere else. The first team had had four managers in 2004 – Gordon Strachan, Paul Sturrock, Steve Wigley and Harry Redknapp – and Harry didn't get the job soon enough to be able to prevent

Southampton being relegated from the Premier League on the last day of the 2004–05 campaign.

That was an awful day. There were people in tears everywhere at St Mary's, even in the press box, apparently. I was at the ground, watching in a suit and tie from an executive box, when Southampton lost to Manchester United and West Bromwich Albion completed their great escape to stay up. For Southampton, it was the start of a dark period in their history.

I left school that summer, the summer Southampton went down, and at the age of sixteen moved into The Lodge ready for the start of the 2005–06 season. I suppose that was the year my childhood finished. Suddenly, my life after school seemed full of endless possibilities.

Seven

I loved it at The Lodge. Of course I'd been going there off and on for a little while so it wasn't as if it was a big shock to my system to move away from home. I was excited more than anything. Excited about playing football full time. Excited about trying to make it at Southampton and maybe pushing for a place in the first team. When I moved in, I had no idea how fast things would move.

I shared a room with Gareth Bale, who has become a huge star at Spurs and won the PFA Player of the Year Award for the 2010–11 season. We had a real laugh. Some of the lads who lived in the twelve rooms in that redbrick building are still among my closest friends. Gareth and I keep in touch regularly. He came to my twenty-first birthday party, even though he was the only Spurs player in a room full of

Arsenal. It's funny how our careers have taken both of us to north London. We reminisce about the times we had at Southampton like we are old hands. Jake Thomson, who went out on loan to Torquay United a while back, reminded me not so long ago that I'd occasionally put pants on my head as if they were a mask and call myself the Underwear Bandit. Then I'd rush into someone else's room and hit them with a towel. You'll have to forgive me for that: I was only sixteen. Those days in digs are a footballer's equivalent of going to university, I suppose.

Jake says now that the only thing that has changed about me since those days is the size of my wallet. But I had to start adapting early at Southampton. Even as I was getting to grips with living away from home I was also beginning to train with the first team. Sometimes Harry Redknapp got me practising with the senior professionals and sometimes I'd be with the youth team.

In that summer of 2005 I travelled with the first team on the coach up to Scotland for a pre-season tour. I was sitting in my seat, minding my own business, listening to my iPod, when I was suddenly aware of someone standing in the aisle next to me. I looked up and it was Dennis Wise, whom Harry had signed to try to steady the team and add a bit of experience after we had been relegated.

Dennis had a reputation, obviously. Everyone knew about the various scrapes he had got into over the years. He was one of the hard men of the English game, one of the Crazy Gang at Wimbledon; he was mates with Vinnie Jones and he never shirked a tackle or a challenge. There was something about him. He wasn't really someone you wanted to mess with.

I didn't know what he wanted but I heard him saying something as I looked up at him. I took my earphones out and he repeated it: 'Go and make the lads a cup of tea, Theo.'

'No,' I said, and put my earphones back in.

I had no idea what would happen next, but Dennis didn't say anything. He just walked away. I didn't want to be rude or behave like a stroppy kid. And I didn't refuse out of lack of respect or anything like that. It was just that I was there to play football. I wasn't there to make a cup of tea for people. I wasn't there to be a waiter. I didn't want to be walking down the bus with hot cups of tea when the bus was going hell for leather up the M1.

When my mum heard about it she said I'd probably done it because I'd never made a cup of tea in my life. But the whole thing created a bit of a stink. Dad got a telephone call from the club about it at work. The bloke who called him said there had been some 'trouble' on the team bus that he thought Dad should be aware of. Dad took my side, obviously, and that was the end of it.

I was a little bit worried about it because Dennis had a reputation for exacting retribution on people who crossed him, but he obviously didn't consider me important enough. I was a slight kid. I wouldn't have been much of a challenge for him. I don't know, maybe part of him respected me for not doing what he had asked me to do.

I only had one other brush with Dennis. A couple of months later I was booting a ball against some wooden boards at the training ground at Staplewood. After a few kicks and rebounds, I whacked the ball again and mishit it. It missed the boards and smashed through the glass windows behind them where the gym was and where Dennis was doing some work on the exercise bike. A couple of seconds later Dennis came running round the corner in a fury. He stood staring at the shattered glass and yelled, 'Who the fuck has done this?' He had shards of glass all over his legs and he was absolutely livid. I was scared rigid but I managed to put my hand up very timidly to signal that I was the one responsible. His demeanour changed straight away. 'Don't worry about it, Theo,' he said, and walked back inside.

I had been half expecting him to grab me by the

collar and give me a piece of his mind, so his reaction was a real relief. For some reason I must have worked my way into his good books by then. I think it was because I was a quiet lad and I didn't come into training being all Billy Big Time. I just got on with my football and I wasn't taking any notice of the publicity I was getting. I think he respected that.

Dennis was part of a soap opera that was developing at Southampton. He had been brought in by Harry Redknapp as a senior player at the same time as Dave Bassett, whom Harry wanted to help him with coaching. But there was a feeling that there was tension between Dennis and Kevin Bond, Harry's number two, and it was a slightly uncomfortable atmosphere.

There were other problems, too. The Southampton chairman, Rupert Lowe, had hired Sir Clive Woodward, the former England rugby coach who had won the World Cup in 2003, as the club's technical director, with responsibility for the medical side of things, team support and structure, and individual coaching with the club's academy players. There was a lot of speculation about the relationship between Harry and Sir Clive, and there were rumours that the chairman wanted to groom Sir Clive to become the next manager. The situation caused never-ending controversy. Sir Clive's reputation wasn't at its height then anyway because he had just returned from being in charge of the British and Irish Lions on a troubled tour of New Zealand. And people asked what qualifications a rugby man had to be in a position of power at a football club.

To make matters worse, Sir Clive worked in tandem with a coach he brought to the club called Simon Clifford, an ex-teacher who had made his name fronting a series of Brazilian Soccer Schools that promoted the *futebol de salão* system of playing with a smaller ball on a court smaller than a pitch to place an emphasis on ball skills. Clifford, who was given the title Head of Sports Science, saw himself as a football revolutionary. Apparently, Sir Clive and Rupert Lowe had introduced him to the staff as 'the best soccer coach in the world'. They were going to change football, they said, and mount a challenge to José Mourinho and Chelsea, who were the top dogs at the time. By introducing new training regimes and specialist coaches, which would see players work much harder on their individual skills, they believed they could take Southampton back into the Premier League.

Sir Clive was diplomatic and respectful towards Harry but Clifford seemed to be much more impatient. It appears he had thought he and Sir Clive were going to be running the club and he was furious when he was prevented from working with the senior players. I didn't mind him, really, but I didn't see that much of him. It was hard for him to make any sort of impact because no one wanted to listen to him.

After he left the club, Clifford was scathing about the coaching set-up he had discovered. He said he was more organized coaching Under-9s than Harry Redknapp and Dave Bassett were with the Southampton first team. For their part, Harry and Dave had no time for Clifford and thought he did not understand the game. The two sides regarded each other with intense mutual suspicion and there were times when I felt I was stuck in the middle.

Sometimes I trained under Harry with the first team. More often, I worked with Georges Prost on technique and repetition. Occasionally, I worked with Clifford as part of the academy set-up. Sir Clive and Clifford had radical ideas about the training routines. There was a brief spell when we trained in the morning at seven a.m., then had breakfast, then trained again, had lunch, trained again in the afternoon, and then again in the evening. That all stopped when Martin Cranie did his hamstring and each side blamed the other for working him into the ground. I didn't do too much of that because more and more I was going with Prost and the first team.

Sir Clive was keen to talk to the scholars as soon as

he joined the club. He invited me, Leon Best, Dexter Blackstock, Nathan Dyer and Martin Cranie to his penthouse suite in Southampton once. I suppose he identified us as the future of Southampton and he wanted to get us on side. He talked through all these plans he had. One of them was that he wanted to have a full training session before a match. I told him that wasn't a good idea. He also said he could train someone not to miss a penalty. He kept referring to his days as England rugby coach and he told us how Jonny Wilkinson did it. He said Wilkinson pictured something like a hat in the crowd and then he pictured that hat between the posts and looked at it and imagined it getting bigger and bigger, and then he could hit his target more easily. No one pointed out that Jonny didn't have a goalkeeper to stop his kicks. None of us knew much about rugby and it didn't really translate.

Later, when the rumours began to circulate that I was on the verge of moving to Arsenal, Sir Clive invited me, Mum, Dad and Warwick over to his apartment for dinner. He produced a graph and a Christmas tree thing that projected everything I could achieve. It was very pretty. It was all about his philosophy of the way the game should be played. The pasta was very good that night.

I don't want to be too negative about him. He was

a nice guy and he was incredibly enthusiastic about what he wanted to do and about his role in football. It was just that it was an awfully big leap for him to take and he was trying to do it at a club that was still quite a high-profile place to be. Maybe somewhere lower down the leagues he might have had more of a chance. It was always going to be an uphill battle for him to succeed from scratch at Southampton.

The politics between the two sides did get me down a bit. There was Harry with the first team and Sir Clive and Clifford with the youth set-up, and I was stuck in the middle, both sides trying to recruit me. Because of the rivalry neither of them wanted to give an inch so I ended up training with both, morning, noon and night. Then I'd be playing youth-team matches, reserve matches and first-team matches. I had a lot of energy but I felt like a pawn in a game.

Despite all that, I felt my decision to stay at Southampton rather than head for one of the big clubs at the end of the previous season was being vindicated. A lot of people had thought my chances would be limited when Harry took over at St Mary's and that he would tend to favour experienced players. They thought he would wheel and deal and bring a lot of new players in and that I wouldn't get a chance. But it didn't turn out like that.

When we had a team meeting for the first game of

the 2005–06 season, against Wolverhampton Wanderers at St Mary's on 6 August, Harry put the team up on the board. It went like this: Antti Niemi, Tomasz Hajto, Claus Lundekvam, Darren Powell, Danny Higginbotham, Djamel Belmadi, Matt Oakley, Nigel Quashie, David Prutton, Ricardo Fuller, Kenwyne Jones. It wasn't a bad side. Then he announced the subs. Dennis Wise was among them. So was I.

The club going down had probably done me a favour in a way because a few players had either left or retired, and being in the Championship meant that Harry was more able to take the odd gamble on somebody untried like me. If Southampton had still been in the Premier League, I doubt I would have got much of a look-in and my rise might not have been quite so quick. So the club's troubles gave me my opportunity.

Even though I'd been involved with the first team in the pre-season, the reality of being so close to the starting eleven now that the real action was about to begin was still a bit of a shock. Suddenly I was look-ing at the prospect of playing against opposition like Wolves who had players of the calibre of Paul Ince and Joleon Lescott in their team. The senior pros at Southampton were great, Nigel Quashie in particular. He went out of his way to reassure me and encourage me. He told me that if I made up my mind to enjoy it and play my natural game, I'd be great.

I was still nervous when I took my place on the bench. It was goalless in the first half and for most of the second. Then Harry told me to go and warm up. My heart started pounding but I tried to look calm and collected as I jogged up and down the touchline and did a few stretches. And then he signalled to me and said I was going on.

I went and stood by the fourth official while he lifted the board, but in all the excitement I hadn't realized I was still wearing my training top. 'What about your shirt, Theo?' somebody shouted from the bench. There was plenty of laughter about that. I would have been embarrassed, but there wasn't really time to be embarrassed.

I came on for Kenwyne Jones, whose boots I cleaned, in the seventy-third minute and became the youngest ever player to appear for Southampton, at sixteen years and 143 days old, which beat the previous record set by Danny Wallace, who was sixteen years and 314 days old when he first appeared for the first team in 1982. It was quite a list to be at the top of, actually. After me, the youngest Saints players were Danny Wallace, Allen Tankard, Martin Chivers, Mick Channon, Keith Granger, Martin Cranie and Alan Shearer. Shearer was seventeen years and 229 days old when he made his debut.

Harry told me to just be myself. I did my best. There were more than twenty-four thousand fans at St Mary's and it was an incredible buzz to hear them chanting my name. Mum and Dad were sitting high up in one of the stands and Mum still says she got a bigger thrill from that moment than from anything else I have done in my career with England or Arsenal.

I packed quite a lot into my first seventeen minutes of league football. I ran around like a madman, tackling back, running at players, being fouled. I was dragged down by Lescott on the edge of the box at one point to win a free-kick. There was one run towards the end when I thought I was going to be clean in on goal until I was denied by a last-ditch tackle from Rob Edwards. I got one shot in, too, after a body swerve and a quick dribble, but it was blocked.

The game finished 0–0 and we had Lundekvam sent off soon after I came on. A lot of people had been expecting Southampton to bounce straight back up so it wasn't the ideal start as far as the supporters were concerned. But they seemed to gain quite a lot of consolation from my debut, and the next day the newspapers made a lot of my arrival. Mum filled two scrapbooks just from cuttings of that Wolves game. The *Southern Daily Echo* said: 'Excited on his full debut. Could be great things to come from him.' In the *News of the World*, Rob Beasley wrote, 'All that Harry Redknapp's Saints had to cheer as they scrambled a draw was the first senior appearance of Theo Walcott.' The *Sunday People* headline was 'He's Cott the Lot'. Only the *Sunday Times* kept a more sober perspective. 'Defiant Niemi Halts Wolves' was the headline at the top of their match report.

I watched the highlights of the game over and over again when I got home. I couldn't wait for another chance, but Harry warned the fans and the media not to get carried away. He said he was going to ration the number of matches I played because he didn't want to risk any sort of burn-out. He told them I wasn't going to be the club's saviour just yet.

Eight

Thankfully I didn't just fade back into obscurity after the Wolves game. Harry kept playing me. I came on as substitute in the games at Luton and Sheffield Wednesday and at home to Norwich. After that I was on the bench for some games and not for others. When I was among the substitutes, Harry usually gave me twenty minutes or so at the end. I was enjoying it immensely, even though I was still in a kind of never-never land between the youth team and the first eleven.

For home games it was left up to me how I got to St Mary's so I'd usually grab a lift with one of the scholars who had a driving licence. It was a bit haphazard. Dad came to take me to the stadium one day and wasn't particularly impressed when he found me having beans on toast for my pre-match meal. I was still earning £80 a week, too, plus win bonus. It was as if the club didn't quite know whether to treat me as a man or a boy.

Then, in the middle of October, I made another big breakthrough. Harry pulled me aside after training one day and told me that I was going to be in the starting line-up for the first time for the midweek league match against Leeds United at Elland Road on 18 October. I couldn't wait for the game to come.

I played like I was unstoppable that night. Leeds went 2–0 up inside twenty minutes but then I got a chance and I took it. I had been dashing around for all I was worth since the start, playing up front with Ricardo Fuller. I was up against a big centre-back called Paul Butler who wasn't a spring chicken any more. He was a nice guy, though. We'd only been playing for a few minutes when he stopped to catch his breath, looked up at me and said, 'I'm too old to be playing against people as quick as you, son.' A few minutes after that, someone pumped a long ball over the top from midfield and Butler was desperately trying to stop me running on to it. I got ahead of him and nodded the ball up in the air before it dropped. I watched it all the way down, then volleyed it towards goal.

I got a good connection, but it was straight at the Leeds keeper, Neil Sullivan, who had come off his line. I hit it so well that Sullivan didn't have time to get his body behind it and the ball bounced off the underside of his body as he dived and trickled towards the net. I started to chase it, as did Sullivan and Butler, but after a couple of bounces it was clear that they wouldn't be able to catch it. I watched the ball cross the line then turned away to celebrate. I didn't know what to do. It was a great feeling.

I felt like *I* crossed a line that night. Things began to change for us as a family a little bit. My football career started to have an impact on us. It didn't change things for the worse, but it did change things. My family had always been committed to me making it as a professional but we had fitted it around our lives. There was a change in that dynamic now.

Because Harry had given me good notice that I would be starting at Leeds, Dad had had plenty of time to ask if he could have the day of the game off. He was by now working for the BG Group, an energy supply company, and he told his boss about my situation and that, obviously, he was willing to take the day as part of his holiday allowance. His boss refused the request. She said she had a morning meeting and my dad was needed on site. So Dad asked if he could just have the afternoon off. She refused again, and added that he had to make a choice between watching me play football and the job. So Dad wrote out a resignation letter there and then, gave it to her and walked out. When he phoned Mum to tell her he had chucked in his job, she thought he had gone mad. She pointed out that meant we had hardly any money coming in. He still says it was worth it, though. He got to see my first goal in professional football.

Four days later I started another game and scored again. This time it was against Millwall at the New Den. I intercepted a backpass, took the ball round Andy Marshall, the Millwall keeper, and slid it into the empty net. I got kicked quite a lot by my marker in that game. I've still got the scars, actually. I don't recall the guy's name but he didn't have a lot of teeth. He was proper Millwall. Scary.

But I was actually finding it quite easy to settle in at Championship level. I don't want that to sound arrogant; people like Nigel Quashie were giving me a lot of help, and a lot of the centre-backs in that league were on the slow side. They were experienced, but they were slow. We hit a lot of balls over the top and I'd either run on to them or come short and spin. And I had so much energy then that I was running for fun.

I started the next game against Stoke and scored in that, too. This time I ran on to a brilliant ball that put me clean through on Steve Simonsen, the Stoke keeper, and as he advanced to try to narrow the angle

I slotted the ball low past his right hand and into the net. It was the opening goal in a 2–0 win. That goal felt special because it was my first at St Mary's and the crowd went wild. Three successive starts and three goals. I couldn't believe it.

My little run of form created a bit of a stir. People started putting labels on me like 'the hottest prospect in football' and 'the next Wayne Rooney'. I was talked about as a prodigy, the successor to players like Leon Knight and Joe Cole whose talent had become apparent at a very early age and who had been tipped for greatness almost before they had played a game.

The publicity unsettled a few people at Southampton. Suddenly there were headlines in the paper about how Chelsea were planning a big bid for me. Other clubs were supposed to be interested too. And so Mum, Dad and I were invited to St Mary's for a friendly chat with Rupert Lowe, Harry and Malcolm Elias, the scout who had played such an influential role in bringing me to Southampton in the first place.

The meeting took place in the boardroom and the atmosphere was awkward from the start. Harry's body language wasn't good. He seemed uncomfortable. He kept his arms folded and didn't say much. Rupert Lowe talked quite a lot and it was as if he was trying to court us. We found it all a bit off-putting, really. It was the first time we had had any contact with anyone senior at the club and there was a slightly accusatory air about some of the things they were asking about other clubs.

I loved it at Southampton, but the club to me really meant Georges Prost and the people involved with the academy and the youth set-up. It felt slightly odd that the senior people at the club had never really done anything to make my family feel welcome and now it seemed to us that they were giving us the heavy hand about what I was planning for my future. Until that meeting, Mum and Dad had just come to the first-team games, watched and left. That was fine. It wasn't that we expected anything else. But it was the youth side of things that made it feel like a family club to us, not the first team.

At one point in the meeting Malcolm looked at me and said, 'You are happy here, aren't you?' It felt a bit strong. I'd stayed quiet until then. Their approach had taken me by surprise. So in response I told Malcolm I just wanted to keep on enjoying my football. I didn't know what they were getting at or why they had adopted what felt like a curious approach. I didn't mention anything about being stuck in the middle of the tussle between Harry and Sir Clive. I didn't really see what that would achieve. But Southampton was a soap opera and everyone seemed to be pulling in different directions.

I started every game we played in November, but it wasn't a good month for us. We drew three games and lost to Leeds. We dropped down to twelfth in the table, twenty-one points off the promotion places, which were occupied by Reading and Sheffield United at that stage of the season. And then, on 24 November, Portsmouth sacked their manager, Alain Perrin. Soon there were rumours that they wanted Harry Redknapp to return to Fratton Park, and at the beginning of December he resigned to go back to Pompey.

Even if the situation around him had been confused, Harry had been great for me. He gave me my chance and he wasn't scared of giving other young players an opportunity too. I was sad to see him go. I think the tension between Woodward and Clifford wore him down a bit, and the chemistry between his coaches Dave Bassett and Kevin Bond wasn't quite what it should be. I don't think Harry ever really felt comfortable at Southampton.

Like Gareth Bale, he's sleeping with the enemy now, of course, doing a fantastic job as manager of Spurs. I always say hello to him when I see him at north London derbies and I will always feel grateful to him for having the faith to play me in the

Southampton first team. We don't chat for ages or anything because we've both moved on, but he knows I have a great deal of respect for him.

For a while, Dave Bassett and Dennis Wise took over as joint caretaker managers. I quite enjoyed their time in charge, actually. Bassett made me laugh. In a good way. He was old school but he was fun to play for. And I scored what was probably my best goal for the club under their management, the winner in a 1–0 victory over Luton Town in the middle of December. I chased a long ball down the left, and when the Luton keeper, Dean Brill, rushed out to try to close me down I lobbed the ball over him with my left foot.

Three days before Christmas, George Burley took over. I didn't warm to him, and maybe he didn't warm to me. Having been a regular starter under Harry and Dave I was suddenly in and out of the team. I didn't have too much of a problem with that. I was only sixteen after all. Still, I felt as though some of the momentum I had built up was being taken away.

Burley had a few problems, I think. Sometimes he just wouldn't put in an appearance. And I didn't particularly like his style. Towards the end of my time at Southampton he gave an interview and talked about how he knew my dad really well and had formed a good relationship with him. The thing was, he'd only met him once. I wasn't quite sure what he was trying to prove.

But even though I felt unsettled under Burley's management, the truth is that the decision about my future had effectively been made by the time he became manager. The interest from the top clubs that had wanted to tempt me away from Southampton six months earlier didn't go away, and by the time Burley arrived, there was a lot of speculation that Arsenal, Liverpool, Chelsea and Tottenham were about to make bids for me.

I didn't know much about that at the time, although I did know Liverpool were interested. That was only because they had rung our family house in Compton to try to talk to me. My brother, Ashley, answered, and they thought he was me. He told them twice that they had the wrong brother but the bloke on the other end of the line didn't seem to hear, so in the end Ashley just let him give him his whole spiel, thanked him for his time and ended the conversation amicably. The bloke on the other end of the phone was none the wiser. I never did find out who it was.

I thought about going to Liverpool. They were the team I'd supported as a kid and it was very flattering that they were interested in me. But I also thought it might be a bit far from home for me at that stage of my life and career. Maybe other sixteen-year-olds would have been able to handle it, but I liked the idea of staying in the south. I thought about Spurs, too, because they had a good record of bringing kids through and they were playing attractive football under Jol. I didn't think Chelsea was such a good option though. Warwick was impressed with Mourinho on a personal level. I guess it's probably hard not to be. He's a charismatic man. But we both felt it wasn't really the club's style to nurture kids like me through the system. They were about instant gratification, really. They were buying people left, right and centre, and I still felt it would be easy for me to disappear.

I had doubts about leaving Southampton because in many ways I was happy there. The club had done a lot for me and all my mates were there. It was like a home from home for me. But it was already clear that Burley wasn't a big fan of me and I was unsettled by his arrival and the mixed messages he was giving me about my place in the team. At first he seemed to think Southampton should cash in on me and that Nathan Dyer was a better bet to make it to the big time. He changed his view after I scored a cracker against MK Dons in the FA Cup third round at the beginning of January, but by then it was too late.

When it became evident that Arsenal were serious,

it didn't take me long to make up my mind that I should grab the opportunity to move there. The reasons were simple. Two names: Arsène Wenger and Thierry Henry. I liked everything I knew about Mr Wenger's philosophy of football and the responsibility he gave to young players. He was loyal to his young players, too. He stood by them when people were urging him to spend big money on bringing in veterans. He gave them time and space to breathe and grow. And Henry was my hero. Before him it was Michael Owen, but when Henry burst on to the Premier League scene, I thought everything about him was brilliant. The idea of training with him and learning from him every day was almost too much to hope for. People at school used to joke about how I was going to be the new Thierry Henry. Now I had the chance to work side by side with him.

I didn't get involved with any of the negotiations with other clubs directly. I just wanted to concentrate on playing football. But inevitably things got slightly awkward at Southampton. When it became apparent that Arsenal's interest in signing me was hardening, rumours started flying around and the lads at Southampton were texting me constantly, asking what was going on. I didn't reply to any of them because I didn't want to lie to them; I didn't want to give anything away either. I felt guilty about that.

I didn't really get any stick from the Southampton fans. It all happened too quickly for that. Actually, they were always brilliant to me and, without being too naive, I don't think they begrudged me the opportunity to move to a team like Arsenal. I had a pre-contract agreement with Southampton to sign a professional contract on my seventeenth birthday but it wasn't binding and I'm sure the fans knew that I loved Southampton, it was just that I couldn't turn my back on the chance I was being offered.

There was one incident. That was all. After we beat MK Dons 4–3 in that FA Cup third-round tie on 7 January 2006, where I'd scored the third, Dad and I came out of the main entrance and walked into the car park. It was quite late by then and the place was almost deserted but there was this one guy staring at us pretty intently as we got into the car. It was a bit unnerving. Dad locked the doors but the bloke came right up to the window. He kept grabbing the Southampton badge on his shirt and screaming, 'Stay, stay!' That's what it meant to him.

Burley said later that I should have stayed. He said I left for Arsenal too soon and that I would have benefited from a full season at Southampton. I don't agree. Because things didn't go very well under Burley and the club had a mediocre season and finished mid-table, there was a lot of pressure and tension around.

I don't think playing in those circumstances was particularly good for contemporaries of mine like Gareth Bale.

I played my last game for Southampton against QPR at Loftus Road on 14 January. I played the full ninety minutes. The headline in *The Times* the following Monday morning was 'Disappointing Walcott Outshone by Elders'. Fair enough, I suppose. I didn't have the best game, and we lost 1–0. It was our fifth defeat in six matches. I swapped shirts with Paul Furlong at the end and left the pitch last. I wanted to acknowledge the ovation the Southampton fans were giving me.

After the game, Burley said he was still planning for a future with me at the club. He said a lot of generous things about me too. And he repeated that he thought it would be better for me if I stayed at Southampton for the rest of the season. It was all a bit confusing because around that time Rupert Lowe and Sir Clive Woodward were spotted at the Arsenal training ground at London Colney. They didn't say they were there to discuss me but, given all the speculation, it would have been a bit odd if I hadn't been mentioned.

I didn't know it at the time, but behind the scenes there was still a lot of manoeuvring going on. A couple of clubs were telling Warwick that I should just walk out of Southampton. Because of my age, there was a clause in my contract that would have allowed me to do that. Southampton would take the case to a tribunal and would probably win a few million pounds from the club that had tempted me away. But it would be a lot less than the £10 million or so I was expected to fetch.

At the same time Chelsea had offered £15 million for me, apparently, and Rupert Lowe, understandably, wanted to get the best price possible so he was pushing for me to go to Stamford Bridge. Arsenal weren't willing to match that offer so for a while things got very heated. I had made up my mind I wanted to join Arsenal and nothing was going to shift me. Lowe wanted to get a record deal for me to help his case with supporters who were upset at me going. So it was a difficult time.

In the end, Arsenal agreed to increase their bid to £12 million. That was £7 million immediately and £5 million in add-ons depending on how many games I played for Arsenal, whether I played for England and things like that. It was a two-and-a-half-year deal with a two-year option in Arsenal's favour. Warwick asked me if I wanted to know the details of the personal terms Arsenal were offering, but I told him that I didn't want to know until the move was completed.

A few days after that match at QPR, everything began to jolt into place. Things moved quickly. My mum was shopping with my sister, Hollie, in Reading when she got a call from Dad telling her that we all had to get up to London because the move to Arsenal was on. There was a general sense of panic as well as excitement. We suddenly realized I didn't have any suitable clothes to wear when I was unveiled as an Arsenal player, so on the way to Sopwell House, the hotel Arsenal used to use as a training base, we stopped at a retail park. I bought a brown suit and some brown shoes in a branch of Next. It didn't look as bad as it sounds, but it was all a bit of a rush.

That night we went to the house of the then Arsenal vice-chairman, David Dein, in north London. It had a 1970s feel to it. It was like something out of an Austin Powers movie. Madonna was on the sound system and there was a lot of leopard print. There was me, my mum and dad, Warwick, and one of my other advisers from Key Sports, Colin Gordon. Arsène Wenger was there too. It was the first time I had met him and right from the start I was left in no doubt about his obsession with football.

We had a Chinese meal, then, while Warwick, Colin and Mr Dein were going through the signing document, the Boss and I went into the cinema room at the house and watched Manchester United's FA

Cup third-round replay with Burton Albion. United won 5–0 but there were a couple of incidents that made Mr Wenger throw his arms up in horror. He kept turning to me, talking about things that had happened. It was a real education just watching a game with him.

The next day I had a medical. It was exhaustive. It lasted for more than eight hours. I went to three separate hospitals in London. I had an MRI scan and met with various specialists. Dad panicked because they picked up a problem with my shoulder that went back to the previous October when I had dislocated it in a challenge with Linvoy Primus when I was playing for Southampton reserves against Portsmouth reserves. The medical people at Southampton hadn't diagnosed it as a dislocation, they'd just given me a load of Voltarol anti-inflammatories. But Arsenal's medical was extremely thorough and left little doubt that that was what had happened. Dad was so nervous about the shoulder that he had to go out of the room where I was being examined. He started pacing up and down in the corridor outside. He was phoning all sorts of people. He began to convince himself that the move was going to fall through on medical grounds. He was worried to death. Eventually, though, they gave me the all-clear. All I needed to do now was sign a piece of paper and I was an Arsenal player.

That happened the next day at the training ground. The first person I met when I walked into the complex at London Colney was Thierry Henry. I asked if I could have my photo taken with him. I've still got that picture, and I look absolutely terrified. Robert Pires was there too, and for some reason it seemed even scarier meeting him. Suddenly my brown suit didn't seem quite as sophisticated as I thought it was.

Just before I signed my contract, Mr Dein sat down beside me.

'I presume you know the length of your contract and how much you're being paid,' he said.

I told him I had no idea how much I was being paid.

'What?' he said.

I told him again that I didn't know anything about the money. I had left it to people I trusted.

Mr Dein's face was a picture. But then his surprise turned to a smile.

'You seem to have good people around you,' he said, 'and in a way you're right. Don't worry about the money because the money comes with success.'

Nine

After I signed for Arsenal, Arsène Wenger told me to go on holiday for a fortnight and settle down after all the excitement. I think he was probably envisaging a couple of weeks in the sun, but the reality was we didn't have enough money to go on holiday. Dad had jacked his job in and I had been earning £80 a week so we weren't exactly rolling in it. In the end I borrowed some from Key Sports and took Mel and my family to the Manor House Hotel in Castle Combe to play a bit of golf, chill out and get away from all the attention and speculation that had been coming my way. (Mel doesn't come on my golfing trips any more, by the way. She lets me get on with it with my mates.)

Even then, pre-World Cup, Dad had developed a bit of a thing about the paparazzi, and we'd only just arrived at the hotel when he caused a big commotion. I was playing croquet on the lawn at the front with Mel, Ashley and Mum. Dad was inside, having a quiet drink in the bar. I was vaguely aware of a Japanese bloke, obviously a tourist, taking pictures of the church nearby. Suddenly Dad came charging out of the hotel and started running towards the tourist. He was in Dad-mode, screaming his head off, telling him to stop taking pictures. He got right up to him and demanded to see his camera. The poor bloke, who looked terrified and who obviously had absolutely no idea who I was (apart from the son of a raving lunatic), explained that he was on holiday and was taking pictures of the village. Gradually, Dad began to look very, very embarrassed.

We all got used to me having my picture taken pretty soon. I'd had my photo taken a lot on the day I signed for Arsenal. The club wanted a shot of me with Emmanuel Adebayor and Abou Diaby, who had both joined at the same time as me. It was for the front cover of the Arsenal magazine. I only needed to look at Adebayor and Diaby to know that picture wasn't going to work without a bit of trickery of some sort. They were giants compared to me. I looked like their little boy, not their teammate. So someone from the club brought out a nice thick *Yellow Pages* for me to stand on. That brought me almost up to their shoulders. Dad told me it was the kind of thing they used to do for the Hollywood actor Alan Ladd. He was so small, apparently, they used to dig trenches for his co-stars to walk around in when they had scenes with him so that he would look as tall as them.

Everything was intimidating at first. It was bound to be. When I walked into the changing room at the training ground, it was sparkling clean. Clean like one of those rooms in an advert for kitchen cleaner. The system was that you had to take your shoes off and put sandals on. Adebayor said after he left the club that one of the reasons he didn't get on with Nicklas Bendtner was that Bendtner refused to take his trainers off in the dressing room. (I think it was probably about a little bit more than that.)

The first time I went in there I felt as if everyone was watching me. They were all sitting down in their places, waiting for me to come in. Henry, Dennis Bergkamp, Jens Lehmann, Robert Pires, Freddie Ljungberg, Kolo Touré, Sol Campbell, Ashley Cole . . . I think that's what it must be like when you're the defendant and you walk into a courtroom. I felt my jaw dropping as I looked at all these famous faces. I reached my peg and saw my number 32 shirt there, neatly pressed, waiting to be put on.

The first training session was something else too. I

got the ball with my back to goal and Sol came clattering right through me. That was his way of welcoming me to Arsenal, my alternative formal introduction. It hurt like hell but I was determined not to show it. I didn't want to limp off injured on my first day. I would have lost face if I'd done that. The pain wore off after a while anyway. The adrenalin was pumping round my body like never before.

After training there was shooting and finishing practice against Jens. I did OK. We did a few one-on-ones and I went round him easily the first time I took him on. He wasn't pleased. He got the ball out of the back of the net and booted it away as hard as he could. Shooting didn't go quite as well. I hit quite a few over the bar. After another flew too high, Freddie started laughing and shouted over at me, 'You're not at Southampton now!'

Freddie was often at the centre of things in training. There were plenty of heated moments and a lot of them seemed to involve him. There was nothing quite like the time when he and Olof Mellberg had a scrap with each other in front of the cameras during Sweden's preparations for the 2002 World Cup in Japan and were writhing around on the ground. But there were often heated words. There were feuds, too. You'd see someone who had gone down under a heavy challenge from a teammate waiting for their opportunity to exact revenge. They'd stroll around, not really interested, until the guy they were gunning for got the ball. Then they'd spring into action. It's normal. Professional footballers are competitive animals. Everybody wants to win. Even in training.

Training at Colney was like being educated at the best school in the country. It was beautiful just to be on the same pitch as some of those guys. I loved watching Bergkamp, in particular. When I look back on those first few months at Arsenal now, I realize how lucky I was to have been on the same pitch as him, even for a short time. It turned out to be his last season at the club and his last in football before he retired. What a player he was. He didn't run very much by the time I was sharing a training pitch with him but he still stood out. It was his touch and the way he got other people involved. It was like watching a magician.

And then there was Thierry. He helped me a lot from the start. It would be an overstatement to say that he took me under his wing, but again, just being around him was an education for a kid like me. I knew when I was weighing up my options before I signed that it was possible he would leave at the end of the season, but I figured that even if I only got to train with him for six months it would still be a priceless part of my education as a footballer.

Thierry was so tall and powerful and everything seemed to be so easy for him. There was one occasion when he tried to teach me and Ashley Cole a trick. He talked Ashley through what he was going to do, running at him down the touchline and lifting the ball over his foot when he tried to tackle him. Even though he had told Ashley what he was going to do, Ashley couldn't get anywhere near him when he actually did it. Thierry told me to try to do it, but for some reason it didn't work quite as well when I tried it. I was very much a work in progress.

My arrival at Arsenal coincided with a period of great change at the club. My signing generated plenty of talk about the future, but a lot of things were coming to an end as well. For a start, it was the club's final season at Highbury after ninety-three years there, and the place was awash with nostalgia and a sense of history. The season I joined, we wore burgundy shirts instead of the traditional red shirts with white sleeves because those were the colours the team played in during their first season at Highbury in 1913–14. Everyone knew Bergkamp would be leaving, too, and then there was the speculation about Thierry's future. Mind you, there was always speculation about Thierry's future. There was always someone who wanted to try to tempt him away from Arsenal, but the bond he had with the Boss and the fact he was so happy with the way the team played its football seemed to be enough to keep him at the club. I looked to him as an example of someone who made his decisions based on the right priorities. I wanted him to stay for as long as possible. I loved being around a player who was my football hero.

Thierry left in the end, of course, at the close of the 2006–07 season when he signed for Barcelona, but he's still a hero of mine. He came back to The Emirates in October 2009 to watch us play Blackburn Rovers and it was a real honour to wear the number 14 shirt that he used to wear, with him watching from the stands. We won the game 6–2 and after the match I got him to sign the shirt. It's on the wall at home now next to the one he signed for me when I first joined.

Thierry gave me my first proper Arsenal nickname. Whenever I went into the dressing room in my second season at the club, he'd shout out 'Lewis!', which was enough to make all the other players crack up laughing. Thierry thought I looked like Lewis Hamilton, who burst on to the scene in Formula One at the start of 2007. I couldn't see it myself but it made the rest of the lads happy. Still, 'Lewis' was an improvement on my other nickname. 'Sweet Little Boy,' they'd say when I walked into the dressing room, because I was baby-faced and clean-shaven. I had to grow a beard to get rid of that one.

These days I don't really have a nickname at Arsenal any more. When Sol Campbell came back to the club in the 2009–10 season he started calling me Lewis again, mainly when he wanted to wind me up about something. Other than that Lewis doesn't seem as popular any more. Maybe it's because Lewis Hamilton isn't quite as popular as he was when he first broke into F1. Some of the guys call me 'T'. My dad calls me 'TJ'. That's about it.

I was included in the first-team squad for the Premier League game against Birmingham City at the beginning of February and the Boss talked up my chances of playing. But I didn't get on. I did make my first appearance in an Arsenal shirt a couple of days later, though, for the reserves. Inevitably, it was against Portsmouth, the bitter rivals of my old club, Southampton. We lost the game but I scored late on, smashing a right-foot half-volley past Sander Westerveld at close range. It was a good start.

I scored my first 'home' goal for the reserves against Charlton Athletic at Barnet's ground, Underhill, in March, and by then I'd also scored on my debut for the England Under-19s. The Boss was starting to tease the media about how Sven-Göran Eriksson should pick me in the England squad, but Arsenal had players coming back from injury and I didn't quite do enough to get back on to the bench again that season.

The Boss said he hadn't used me because he never found himself in a situation where he could afford to take a risk. That season, Arsenal went all the way to the Champions League Final and were locked in a desperate battle for fourth place in the Premier League with Spurs. At one stage it looked as though we would have to rely on beating Barcelona in the final to get back into the Champions League the following season. So rather than gamble with me, the Boss turned to players like José Antonio Reyes, Robin Van Persie and Bergkamp.

On the last day of the season, in Arsenal's last ever game at Highbury, we needed to beat Wigan Athletic and hope that Spurs didn't beat West Ham at Upton Park. The Spurs team came down with food poisoning the night before the game and lost 2–1. And we gave Highbury a fitting send-off: Thierry scored a hat-trick in a 4–2 win, which meant that he was the Premier League's top scorer with twenty-seven goals and that we clinched fourth place. As the fans and the players said goodbye to the stadium, Thierry knelt and kissed the grass.

I'd still had some great experiences, though. The Champions League run to the final in Paris was a brilliant adventure. We beat Real Madrid on the way and I was on the bench at the Bernabéu, which was awe-inspiring. What a stadium that is. So steep-sided and traditional. You could feel the history cascading down from all its tiers. The people in the crowd looked like dots against the night sky.

Of course I didn't travel with the team to Paris for the final because I'd been called into the England World Cup squad by then. I watched the game with some of the lads at our training camp on the Algarve, over a Chinese takeaway. It was a tense final, particularly after Jens Lehmann was sent off early on for a professional foul. But I thought we might still do it when Sol Campbell headed us into the lead. We held them off and held them off, and Thierry was unlucky not to put us further ahead, but eventually Barcelona's greater numbers told and they scored two late goals to win the game. Juliano Belletti got the winner.

I was desperately disappointed for my teammates but I felt detached from it all as well, partly because I had hardly been involved with the Arsenal first team, and partly because I was sitting in a villa on the Algarve doing everything I could to settle into the England World Cup squad. Sometimes, in that first year with Arsenal and England, it felt as if my whole life was about trying to fit in, trying to prove myself.

I wasn't given a chance to do that in Germany, and

when I got back to England after the tournament many people thought I would just fade away. Some of them seemed to expect that I would never be heard of again, that I had had my fifteen minutes of fame and that I was just some sort of trick of the light. Even some of those who knew a bit more about the situation and realized I was a player of real potential harboured fears for me. A number of people thought I would have real problems dealing with coming home from the World Cup without having played a single minute of football. Some were branding me a failure because Mr Eriksson hadn't picked me. They were trying to turn me into some sort of joke figure, the little kid whose big adventure had gone horribly wrong.

There was a chance, obviously, that my career might start to go backwards. The fact that Mr Eriksson had included me in the squad had made me a lot more visible, a lot more high-profile. There was a lot of pressure on me when I got back to England because everyone was waiting to see if there was any substance to this kid who people were now saying had been selected for the World Cup on the foolish whim of a desperate manager. My opportunity to do my growing up as a footballer out of the spotlight had disappeared for ever. I couldn't now learn on the undercard of a bill, like a young fighter

Left: Starting out: Aged eleven, with my dad, Don, and with my hands on some silverware.

Below: I scored six goals on my debut for AFC Newbury and more than a hundred times in one season. Needless to say, we won every game and tournament we played in.

WALKERS

THEALE TIGERS
6-A-SIDE
Tournament
May 28th - 29th 2000

My teacher at school got us to draw a timeline of how we imagined the rest of our lives. I saw myself scoring a hat-trick on my debut for Southampton, winning the World Cup and then going on to manage Liverpool, who I supported.

Get a lot of money from wages at club.

Win the world cup with England and win the premership with Southampton.

Debut for Southampton F.C. scoring a hatrick against Liverpool f.c. who I support.

Get married and have a beautiful wife and have happy years.

Have a baby with my engaged wife and then move into my mansion.

Get first car which is a Lotus Elite

Playing football for Newbury scoring 77 goals then going to Southampton Academy

Kindergarten school then moving to primary

Born & have first birthday

BIRTH

secondary school, great but someone bullied me.

playing primary football at Coca cola club.

Boring lazy years.

Old boring life
at 40 years
old.

Retirement
from football but
manage Liverpool
F.C and win trophy's.

Go abroad to
Jamaica.

Get a house
in Jamaica
but is a small
bungalow.

Win the lottery
and by everything
I want as an
old man.

wife die's
at the age
of 85.

Sad Life
at the
age of
85 to

95 then...

I die but have
grave next to my
DEATH wife.

Meeting my hero, Michael Owen, when I was a ballboy at Chelsea v. Liverpool in April 2000. Who would have thought that I'd come on as substitute for him when I made my England debut six years later?

I also got to meet Robbie Fowler (**above**) and Jamie Redknapp (**below**) that day at Stamford Bridge. Jamie's dad, Harry, gave me my football-league debut for Southampton.

Proud to be a Saint: I scored a hat-trick against Chelsea Under-13s in one of my first matches for Southampton.

Right: 6 August 2005: My first-team debut for Southampton against Wolves. I packed a lot into my first seventeen minutes of league football.

Left: Scoring at St Mary's was an even bigger thrill. This goal against Stoke made it three goals in my first three games – not a bad start!

Below: This strike against Luton in December 2005 was one of my best goals for the Saints – a left-foot lob over their keeper, Dean Brill.

Young Gunner. Right from the start
Mr Wenger made me feel at home.

making his way through the ranks. I was still a raw novice but I had to accept that I was also one of the headline acts. It didn't matter whether I liked it or not. I just had to get on with it.

I was determined that I wouldn't shrivel under the pressure. When I got back to training with Arsenal, I gave it everything straight away. The other lads were great with me. There wasn't even much banter about the World Cup. For once, there wasn't really any teasing about how England had done or how I must have splinters in my backside from sitting on the bench for so long. Footballers are not a particularly merciful or sensitive bunch but I think the Arsenal lads felt sorry for me because, after all the headlines about me being included in the World Cup squad, I hadn't been given the opportunity to play.

Almost as soon as I'd got back to England there was speculation that Arsenal would send me out on loan to a club in the Championship. Watford were one of the teams mentioned as a possible temporary home for me. I suppose that kind of rumour was inevitable when I had been at the club for a while and not made an appearance. But I didn't want to go anywhere and the Boss told the press that he didn't want me to go either. He said the rumours were the product of the overactive imagination of the British press.

In fact I did well in pre-season, and when the Boss named the squad for the first league game of the 2006–07 season, against Aston Villa, I was in it. It was our first game at The Emirates, the first game of a new era for the club. For me, too, it felt as if this was a new beginning, a chance to put the doubts other people had about me into the past. A chance to step into the future.

Ten

I was learning so much, so fast. I was learning the Arsenal Way. I was learning how the club reaches the finished product that football purists rave about. I thought my technique was OK before I arrived at Arsenal, but in those first few months at the club and now, at the start of my first full season, I realized that I had a long way to go before I could compare myself with some of the players who were already there.

There's no particular secret to the way we play, but the one thing that strikes me about our routines in training is that we always play on tight pitches. It's very rare that we train on a full pitch. It's usually narrow and short. It puts technique at a premium. One bad touch and someone from the other side is on you straight away. There's no room for error.

The other thing, which complements that, is that

we rarely have what we call an 'all-in' game in training. That is, we don't play a normal match where you can take as many touches as you want. Mostly, we play a system where you can take a maximum of two touches if you're going forward and one touch if you're going back.

That doesn't particularly suit me. It doesn't play to my strengths. My game is more about running at people, dribbling with the ball and crossing it. But I know that the training regime at Arsenal helps me immensely. I noticed an improvement in my technique and my touch in those first few months because of that emphasis on controlling the ball fast and finding a teammate straight away.

The funny thing is that it isn't as if the Boss is constantly screaming at everyone to play it short and never play a long ball. It's just that everyone knows the underlying philosophy is pass and move, pass and move, so the players at the club seem to do it automatically. Everybody interlinks and changes positions. It just happens. It's amazing to watch and even better to be a part of. There are some pretty hefty tackles too, of course, but on a small pitch everyone works harder to find space; and then when you get out to the bigger pitch, it feels so much easier. That's why we play such great football.

I loved the atmosphere at the club straight away,

even though it was a time of some upheaval and considerable change. Influential players had left the club by the time I got back from the World Cup. As well as Bergkamp and Pires having gone, José Antonio Reyes had returned to Spanish football, on loan at Real Madrid, Sol Campbell had gone to Portsmouth, and Ashley Cole had gone to Chelsea.

Ashley's move had created a furore. Chelsea finally signed him on transfer deadline day at the end of August 2006, in part exchange for William Gallas. Chelsea claimed William had threatened to score an own goal if he didn't get his move away, which he denied. All in all, things seemed to get pretty fraught. Ashley's transfer was one of the longest-running sagas in English football's recent history. It had dragged on since January 2005, when he and his agent had met the then Chelsea manager, José Mourinho, in a London hotel to discuss a move and news of the meeting had subsequently appeared in the newspapers.

There was a great deal of bitterness between the two clubs about it. Not for the first time or the last, Chelsea were accused of thinking that their riches allowed them to trample proper procedures into the ground. But, as is the way with footballers, there wasn't really much talk about it among the Arsenal players. It certainly didn't alter the atmosphere in the dressing room that much. I don't think footballers chat as much about transfers as people might think, certainly not when we're together and in a playing situation. People are left to get on with it. There was an assumption that Ashley's move must have caused a great deal of bitterness between the players of Chelsea and Arsenal, but it didn't. Not really. The Arsenal fans hated Ashley for what he did, but as his teammates we felt no resentment towards him.

There was a bit of banter. One day I was training with Ashley and Thierry was teasing him about some of the stuff that had come out in Ashley's auto-biography. I hadn't read all the details about the negotiations between Arsenal and his agent over his pay demands but I was vaguely aware he was getting some stick in the media about a passage where he said he nearly crashed his car when he was told Arsenal were only offering him £55,000 a week. Thierry was poking fun at him for something to do with that and a few people joined in. But it was all very light-hearted. There was, as I said, no bitterness so far as the players were concerned over Ashley's move. People may have wanted him to stay for the good of the club's performances on the pitch but foot-ballers tend not to get involved in their teammates' business. It's up to each player to know what's best for his own career. So the mood at Arsenal didn't change at all. All the players knew he was going and Ashley just kept his head down and got on with his job.

Ashley was a very loud player in the dressing room, very confident. He and Sol were close mates. They were both bubbly characters and they were very influential among the group. Ashley was a terrific full-back too. He still is. I played against him a few times in training. He was hard to play against because he has great pace and fantastic energy. It was a bit like playing against Patrice Evra, really. Ashley was non-stop. I had to think about defending against him as much as trying to attack him. He was very similar to the way Gaël Clichy is now. Gaël probably learned a lot from Ashley.

I wasn't close mates with Ashley. He and I are very different. On the pitch he is a great player, but off the pitch he has to deal with a lot of pressure.

I wouldn't want to be him. I wouldn't be able to deal with it. I don't like the limelight away from the pitch. I don't like being stopped in the street or anything like that. I just like to have a quiet life and have fun when I can. Perhaps some of it depends on where you have grown up. If my childhood had been in London, like Ashley's was, maybe I would have been totally different. But I grew up out of the way, in the sticks in Berkshire, with my family, and that kept me under control. I wasn't exactly a streetwise kid. So London life was foreign to me. Ashley is a London boy. He came up through the ranks at Arsenal and I'm sure those guys in the youth team all stuck together just like we did when we were at Southampton. But there's an awful lot less going on in Southampton than there is in London. I've got a lot of respect for everything Ashley has done in the game, but the two of us are just from different backgrounds.

Now and again, people try to make an issue of the fact that there are very few English players in the Arsenal squad, but it has never bothered me. I suppose it was quite a big change that summer when both Sol and Ashley left, but I never felt like a stranger at the club or anything like that. Part of the deal at Arsenal, part of the reason you go, is that it's a mix of cultures and styles gathered together under one umbrella, all trying to play great football.

It's not as if there aren't English lads at the club now anyway. Craig Eastmond, who can play midfield or full-back, is an English player who has come through the youth ranks into the first team squad. Jack Wilshere, who has become an integral part of England's plans, is another graduate of the Arsenal Academy. Kieran Gibbs might have been challenging for a place in Fabio Capello's 2010 World Cup squad if he hadn't broken his foot midway through the season. Defenders Thomas Cruise and Kyle Bartley both have a Champions League appearance to their names. There's others too, even if they sometimes have to go out on loan first. Jay Emmanuel-Thomas, Henri Lansbury and Sanchez Watt have all made a mark playing for clubs in the Championship. And Nicklas Bendtner speaks the language so well he's practically English.

It's nice to have a few English guys around, but it's just as important to have diversity. I've got a few video clips on my phone of Emmanuel Eboué and Alexandre Song doing this dance they do every day in the changing rooms at the training ground. They stick some African music on loud and just start jiving away. They're brilliant. Sometimes, Song does a different dance that involves putting an F1 driver's helmet on his head. Eboué wears a suit for that one. It sounds mad, and it is. They crack me up completely.

The thing that really binds us is nothing to do with nationality anyway. The glue at Arsenal is the football and the loyalty that the Boss shows towards his players, particularly his young players. I know that other clubs have very successful youth policies and that Manchester United's phenomenal run of success was built on the foundation of a crop of young players who came through the ranks in the early 1990s, but I don't think any club has stayed more true to its young players than Arsenal.

The Boss is criticized sometimes for not making forays into the transfer market and splashing tens of millions of pounds on a star striker or a veteran midfield player. Perhaps there have been times when it would have been useful for us to be able to draw on a superstar forward or a big-name defender, but it's also important to remember that we would lose something intangible if we did that, too.

It's not as if he never buys players, it's just that he backs his judgement with the youngsters he brings to the club. And he backs the ability of his staff to nurture those players to the point where they are challenging for a place in the first team. We don't spend the same amount of money as Chelsea, Manchester United, Liverpool and Manchester City but we're still consistently in the top four in the Premier League and challenging for honours.

Every time we have meetings, the Boss always stresses to us the belief he has in the whole squad. That happens even after we've had defeats. In fact, it happens especially after we've had defeats. He makes sure that the pressure is on his shoulders, not ours. The only pressure on us is to try to justify his faith in us. He has so much belief in us and we have to repay him by winning enough matches to start collecting trophies again.

Eleven

I didn't start the game against Aston Villa, Arsenal's first match after I came back from the World Cup. That really would have put me under the spotlight straight away. The Boss brought me on for Freddie Ljungberg after seventy-three minutes. It was eight months since I'd joined the club but finally I felt like a real Arsenal player. I ran out in front of sixty thousand people with the team 1–0 down, desperate to make a mark on my debut and stop that first game at our new stadium ending in the anti-climax of defeat.

It went better than I had dared to hope. I got into the game straight away and felt full of confidence. I went past someone with a trick almost immediately and started a move that ended with Emmanuel Eboué hitting the crossbar. Then, six minutes from the end,

I clipped in a cross from the left, Robin Van Persie nodded it down and Gilberto Silva smashed it past Thomas Sorensen for the equalizer.

What a feeling that was. What a feeling of joy and relief. At last I could draw a line under everything that had happened at the World Cup. I might have felt a bit out of my depth in Germany but I never lost faith in my ability. I was still a very confident kid and I was sure I could prove I was worth a place in the first team to Arsenal fans when the Boss gave me the chance. The impact I made on the Villa game vindicated that belief.

Even though I didn't feel under tremendous pressure going into the game, the way I played did give me a sense of release. Suddenly, people stopped talking about me as if I was some sort of circus freak, the kid who should never have gone to the World Cup. It went back to the way it was when I was at Southampton. People started talking about me as a youngster full of potential again.

The funniest thing was that a few journalists even said that maybe Mr Eriksson had been right to take me to the World Cup after all. Maybe he should have gone further and played me in Germany, they said. England was in its traditional state of post-World Cup disillusion and after my cameo against Villa, people used the benefit of hindsight to say I might have made a difference had Mr Eriksson had the courage to play me.

I didn't care about any of that any more. I just wanted to play well for Arsenal.

I came on again in the Champions League game against Dinamo Zagreb a few days later and laid on the winner for Mathieu Flamini. I came off the bench in the defeat at Manchester City, too, made a couple more substitute appearances, and then, in the middle of October, made my first start, against Watford at home.

They were all decent steps forward, but my progress was blighted by my shoulder injury. The problem that had first manifested itself when I collided with Linvoy Primus while I was playing for Southampton reserves had flared up again. I started having problems with it all the time. My shoulder was popping out and popping back in. The pain was so bad when it happened that it took my breath away. I couldn't do anything. I had to try to avoid the ball until the agony subsided. It ruined my chances of building up the kind of momentum I needed to press for a first-team place.

I played with it for almost the whole season until finally, in March, I had an operation. But from the start of the season until I went to hospital seven months later it got worse and worse. As well as sending shards of pain through my body every time it popped out, it was mentally exhausting. It was always in my head that it would happen again, and the pain when it did was pretty extreme. Mentally it was very draining knowing that you were only one sudden movement away from a surge of agony.

I started playing with heavy strapping but that wasn't comfortable at all. It helped a little bit but I couldn't really play in that kind of pain. At times I was playing with one arm, effectively. I was too scared to try to push people off with my injured arm just in case it popped out. It wasn't nice at all. The Boss said when I went in for the operation I was only half the player he had signed. It was very debilitating.

The injury affected me, but it didn't totally ruin my season. There were still some great moments, particularly in the Carling Cup, where the Boss made a point of stocking the team with young players. There were some real highs for us in that competition that season. After winning at Everton, in early January we beat Liverpool 6–3 at Anfield, the first time they had conceded that many goals at home for seventy-seven years, with a team that included me, Cesc Fabregas, Julio Baptista, Denilson, Alex Song, Johan Djourou, Jérémie Aliadière, Justin Hoyte and Armand Traoré. It was intoxicating being part of a performance that was all about youth and feeling that we were going to grow into a group of players that would be a match for anyone. That was what the Boss was building towards, trying to mould young players to his way of playing football and allowing them to enjoy the game so much that they wanted to stay with the club when they matured.

We played a full-strength Spurs team in the semi-finals and came back from two goals down to steal a draw in the first leg at White Hart Lane. What a night that was. It was my first appearance in a north London derby and the atmosphere was fantastic. I had never been involved in anything like that. I'd certainly never experienced that kind of hostility before. The closest thing was playing for Southampton at Millwall, which was fairly tasty, but White Hart Lane that night was intense.

The players still appreciate what the derby means to the fans. They know how important it is to the supporters. It's important to the players, too, but I'm sure it's different now to the way it used to be in the 1970s and 1980s when the teams were dominated by English players. Most Arsenal players are not English so they can't fully appreciate the history of the fixture. It would be the easy thing to say they were especially pumped up for the derby but it wouldn't be true. They treat the north London derby the same as any other game – which means they desperately want to win it.

I nearly got a late winner in my first experience of the derby. I waited and waited for a hanging cross from Fabregas to fall to me and I caught it sweetly when it came down but my volley went just wide and the game ended 2–2. It didn't matter. We won the second leg at The Emirates 3–1 after extra time and went through to meet Chelsea in the final. It felt great to beat Spurs in a semi. It felt even better to be in a final.

Chelsea put their full team out at the Millennium Stadium. John Terry, Frank Lampard, Didier Drogba, the lot. José Mourinho, the Chelsea boss at the time, didn't really pursue a youth policy in the same way that Arsène Wenger did. For him, everything was about the here and now. His philosophy was all about winning immediately. He was often scornful about how the Boss could survive at Arsenal without winning trophies. He said he didn't have that luxury.

Anyway, the Boss didn't compromise. Even though it was a final, he selected a team faithful to his Carling Cup policy, a team packed with young players. The average age was under twenty-one, and even though there was pressure to play the likes of Thierry Henry against Chelsea's senior players, the Boss resisted it. I think that as a group the young players at Arsenal were starting to feel almost invincible, and we went out there and gave it everything.

We dominated the game in the opening minutes and I felt full of confidence. I watched a rerun of the match afterwards and it was funny how astonished the commentators sounded about how well we were playing. No one seemed quite able to believe that this team of kids was bossing a Chelsea side of superstars. A lot of people desperately wanted us to win because we were the underdogs, and we fed off some of that emotion.

After eleven minutes we got a corner, and when it was headed out to me about thirty yards out I retrieved it and turned away from Andrei Shevchenko, who was coming to try to tackle me. I was vaguely aware that Shevchenko had fallen flat on his backside because he had been deceived by my change of direction. That made me feel good, and I threaded a pass across the box to Diaby. He played it back to me and I tipped the ball away from Ricardo Carvalho as he lunged in to try to dispossess me. That touch took me past Lampard and JT in one movement and into the Chelsea area, and when Petr Cech rushed out to meet me, I curled my shot round him and into the far corner.

It was my first goal for Arsenal and I went a bit mad. The rest of the players mobbed me but I kept bursting through them like a rugby player breaking tackle after tackle. I hadn't been reading the newspapers but I'd been told I'd been getting some criticism for not scoring. I wasn't too bothered about that because I had been getting plenty of assists. No one knew, either, about my shoulder problem. But it was still a great feeling to hit the back of the net for Arsenal at last.

It was another moment when I felt like I had made a giant step forward. To score in a final was great. No one had expected us to do well in the competition because the Boss had fielded such a young team throughout and that goal felt like a real breakthrough moment, scoring while the nation was watching in a live television game. When I watched footage of the game later, there were pictures of Thierry jumping up and down on the sidelines celebrating my goal.

We couldn't make our advantage stick, though. We lost our rhythm a bit when there was a long break for a terrible injury to John Terry in the second half after he had been knocked out while he cleared a ball with his head. There was a mêlée in their penalty area and Diaby tried to kick the ball but connected with JT's head instead. JT was out cold before he hit the grass. Diaby kicked him so hard he had to go off injured himself a few minutes later. Thankfully, we found out after the game that JT was OK.

Gradually, Chelsea began to come back at us, and two goals from Drogba won it for them. Not before there was a brawl on the pitch right near the end, though. It started when Mikel fouled Kolo Touré and then everybody piled in. Mourinho even came running on to the pitch. At the end of it, Mikel, Touré and Adebayor were all sent off. I stayed where I was on the other side of the pitch. I was standing with Arjen Robben and we were both shaking our heads in disbelief. 'Why is this happening?' Robben said. I don't think he was particularly comfortable with the physical side of the English game.

I got a lot of praise for my goal in the aftermath of the game and most reports talked about the final as if it had been a moral victory for Arsenal because of the promise our young players had shown. It gave me another shot of confidence, but I couldn't really capitalize on it. My shoulder had been getting worse and worse and the strapping the Arsenal physios were putting on it was feeling tighter and tighter, and it got to the point where I couldn't play on with it any more.

Three weeks after the final I came on as a late substitute in a league game at Everton. I fell heavily in their area when I was trying to reach the ball and my shoulder popped out again. The pain felt worse this time and I left the field clutching my arm. It was incredibly frustrating because Thierry and Robin Van Persie were both injured too and I might have got a decent run in the first team. But there was nothing I could do.

I went into hospital the following week for an operation. That was my season over. It also meant I would never play in the same side as Thierry again. There were rumours Barcelona wanted to sign him and I noticed that his behaviour changed a little around the training ground. I think the uncertainty and the tension of the situation were getting to him. I was at the training ground after the season had finished, working on the rehab for my shoulder, and one day I saw him arrive with his daughter and show her round the place. It was like he wanted to show her a place where he had been happy. I realized then that he was going to leave.

Twelve

It had never stopped being a thrill for me to be on the same pitch as Thierry, wearing the same Arsenal shirt he was wearing. He had made me and my family welcome at the club right from the start and I loved playing with him. People said when he had gone that his presence intimidated some of the younger players. I never felt that way personally, but I understand what the comments were trying to get at. Thierry was a perfectionist. He demanded the highest standards and he didn't try to hide his displeasure if someone fell short.

There's nothing wrong with that. In fact, it's a sign of a great player. But sometimes I could see that it inhibited a few of our players. Not just the young ones, actually. If Alexander Hleb, who was keeping me out of the team, did something wrong, Thierry would kill him and Hleb just went into his shell. When Thierry left, Hleb started playing his best football.

Thierry was stern with the younger players as well. When they got the ball they wanted to do the simple thing rather than try anything risky in case it went wrong, and they got criticized for it. A lot of the time they just gave the ball straight to Thierry. Some lads were relieved when he went and it gave the new generation of players at Arsenal the confidence to step up and stride forward. Hleb and Cesc, in particular, took on a lot more responsibility when Thierry went.

I was sorry he left. I thrived on being around a great player like him, someone whose style I admired and whose achievements I was in awe of. I still look up to him and still think about what he did at Arsenal. I now wear the same shirt he wore and I'd like to be able to give the fans at least some of the same type of excitement that he provided for them. I saw the standing ovation he got at the end of our Champions League quarter-final with Barcelona when he came back to The Emirates for the first time. That is quite a thing to be able to inspire that kind of loyalty in people and to retain it even when you have moved on.

I was fully fit by the start of the 2007–08 season but I was still in and out of the team. I started some games and wasn't even on the bench for others. There was a lot of competition to get into the first eleven and even though the manager had talked a lot about playing me up front, I was behind Adebayor, Van Persie and Eduardo in the pecking order. Maybe Bendtner as well.

It wasn't that much easier to break in on the flanks. Hleb started the season brilliantly and Tomas Rosicky had the right wing nailed down. Diaby and Denilson were in the mix too, and sometimes Van Persie would be used out wide as well. I knew how good all those players were and I knew I was still only eighteen but I grew increasingly frustrated about not being able to hold down a place no matter how well I played when I came off the bench.

I did start the game against Derby County at The Emirates in September, but even though we won 5–0 I knew I hadn't had a good game. In fact I was so bad my dad wouldn't even speak to me after the match. For once I just needed a few platitudes from him. Even though I would have known they weren't true, they might have made me feel a tiny bit better. But all I got was silence. He didn't trust himself to speak, apparently, because he was so disappointed with my performance. My mum says he's an absolute nightmare to sit with in the box at home games. He gets absurdly worked up.

A few months into the season I went to see the Boss to tell him that I was getting frustrated with my lack of opportunities. I didn't go to see him in his office, I just went up to him when he was standing on the touchline at the training ground and asked him exactly what I had to do to get a start. He said he wanted me to be more aggressive. He said he felt I had been playing with my handbrake on since my shoulder operation and he wanted me to take the handbrake off. He said he thought I was still trying to protect my shoulder.

The next game was a home tie against Slavia Prague in the Champions League. I was in the starting line-up and I scored twice. Pretty good timing. There were other reasons why I wanted to do well that night. Luke Amos, the brother of my sister's partner Ryan, had been killed in a motorbike accident on a country lane a couple of weeks earlier and I wanted to make a gesture of support and remembrance, however small. Ryan was at the game that night, so when I scored my first goal I pointed my fingers up to heaven.

We were top of the table at Christmas, but because I was still in and out of the team there was a new series of stories during the January transfer window that I was going to be loaned out to another club. The Boss was quoted as saying that I was 'not where I would like him to be' and that fuelled the speculation, but I knew the idea of me going out on loan was rubbish.

Suddenly, all sorts of people were offering up their opinions on where it had all gone wrong for me and what I needed to do to get my career back on track. I wasn't really aware that it was off track. David Bentley, who had left Arsenal because he wasn't getting enough first-team action, felt the need to advise me that I ought to leave. 'Sometimes you need football, you need games to become better, to put your skills out on the football pitch,' Bentley said. 'If Walcott is not getting the minutes at Arsenal, he's going to have to look elsewhere. Your career doesn't start and end at Arsenal. It can flourish somewhere else. At the end of the day you want to make a career for yourself. You want to play football for a start and you want to make money as well. It's your job. If you want to make a career for yourself you can't afford to stay at a club where you might be twenty-four or twenty-five with thirty games under your belt.'

That was all fine, but I was only eighteen and I had already played more than thirty games for Arsenal, so by Bentley's reckoning I was about seven years ahead of schedule. Bentley's career hasn't exactly flourished since he left Arsenal either, unless you count not being able to get into the Birmingham City first team last season as flourishing. The Boss was annoyed by him poking his nose in, but it didn't particularly bother me.

Of course I got frustrated now and then, but I'm a patient person. I knew I still had plenty to work on, particularly my left foot and my ability in the air, and I knew that there were some very talented players ahead of me. But it did also feel as though some people expected too much of me, probably because of my price tag when I arrived and the fact that I had been part of the World Cup squad. They expected me to go past someone every time I got the ball while I was trying to learn that often the best thing to do is the simple thing.

In the new year, my dad distinguished himself again. He was willing to try anything to get me to score more goals, and after we were once again drawn against Spurs in the semi-finals of the Carling Cup, he said that if I hit the net in the first leg at The Emirates he'd wear a Captain America suit to the next game. It was total coincidence, obviously, but I did score. I got an equalizer eleven minutes from time when Lee Young-Pyo tried to tackle me and the ball ricocheted off me and past Radek Cerny.

So for the home game against Birmingham on 12 January, Dad wore the outfit as promised. He got some very strange looks up in the executive box area.

They're not used to fancy dress on match day up there. I made sure the club photographer knew exactly where he was going to be as well, so there was a picture of him looking like a muppet in the Arsenal magazine the next week. It just goes to show you should never bet on your kids not succeeding.

There were no smiles when we played Birmingham away just over a month later, though. That match was one of the bleakest games I've ever been involved in, one of the worst experiences of my life. We were still top of the Premier League when we went to St Andrew's on 23 February. I scored two goals in that game, the first two league goals of my Arsenal career, but they were utterly insignificant that day. That day was the day the title race turned against us, and when Eduardo suffered one of the most horrific injuries English football has ever seen.

He was caught by a late tackle by Martin Taylor early in the game. Taylor was sent off and there was a lot of criticism of him afterwards, but I don't think it was a malicious challenge. In the immediate aftermath of the game the Boss said that Taylor should never be allowed to play football again, but he took the comments back later. It was just that Eduardo was too quick for him and Taylor wasn't good enough to get the ball. Taylor caught him full on the shin and Eduardo's left foot was pinned to the ground while his body carried forward. The motion broke his leg in a grotesque way and left him writhing on the ground in agony.

I was on the opposite side of the pitch but I knew it was bad as soon as it happened. I could see Cesc's face and Hleb's face and I just knew. I didn't want to go anywhere near it. It was terrible. (We didn't know it then, but two years later we would have to face the same horror when Aaron Ramsey's leg was shattered by a tackle from Stoke defender Ryan Shawcross.) After nearly ten minutes of treatment, Eduardo was carried off the pitch on a stretcher with an oxygen mask on his face and taken to Selly Oak Hospital.

The rest of us were in shock. It killed us all. We were just thinking about Eduardo for the rest of the first half. He's a very popular lad in the dressing room and everyone was deeply affected. At half-time the Boss told us we had to forget about it and try to win the game for him, and in the second half we went at them and got our heads together. My first goal was a poacher's goal from a corner. For the second one, I ran at the defenders and whacked it in the bottom corner. I was pleased, obviously, but it didn't really feel like the time to celebrate.

Then, right near the end of the match, we conceded a late equalizer. Gaël Clichy made a mistake, Birmingham won a penalty, and our captain, William

Gallas, lost it totally. He started booting advertising hoardings and sat down by the side of the pitch as James McFadden prepared to take their penalty. It wasn't great to see Gallas doing that. It added to a sense of chaos and despair, and I think although he later apologized he lost a bit of respect from other players for the way he behaved. McFadden scored from the spot and the game was drawn.

After the game, it was as though we had lost. I was pleased about my goals but because of Eduardo I didn't really know what to think. Gallas went very quiet and kept himself to himself. It felt like we were so close to winning the Premier League and I think maybe Gallas, with all his experience, realized that that match at St Andrew's could be a turning point. If he did, he was right. We only won once in the next seven league games and that was a bad enough run for Manchester United to overtake us.

We were already out of the FA Cup so our main focus quickly became the Champions League. We had a big night at the San Siro in the second leg of our second-round tie against AC Milan after we had drawn 0–0 at The Emirates. Milan were the reigning champions and they were favourites to go through after their result in north London but we totally out-played them in Milan. Fabregas had one of his best matches for Arsenal. That was the night when it became obvious to everyone that he was a world-class player up there with the very best in the game. Still, despite Cesc's performance and our general superiority, the match was goalless midway through the second half. The worry remained that we wouldn't make our domination count and that they might suddenly conjure a goal out of nothing. The Boss told me to warm up, and with twenty minutes to go he brought me on for Emmanuel Eboué.

It was a great experience playing in that stadium and I was determined to make my mark. Milan were a fine side but they were an ageing side as well and I ran at them as soon as I could. I knocked Kaká off the ball at one point and he fell on to the turf as I shrugged him off. I enjoyed that because my girlfriend, Mel, loves Kaká. I even got his shirt after the game and kept it for myself, which annoyed her immensely.

For someone like me who was still learning the game, it was a real buzz being on that pitch with those Milan players. I will always consider it a privilege to have played against Paolo Maldini in his last game in European competition, and Kaká is a magnificent player. I like everything about the way he goes about his game. He's a class act (although I never say that in front of Mel). Andrea Pirlo was in the side too, and Rino Gattuso and Alessandro Nesta.

I mean, the team was packed with famous names.

It would have been easy to feel intimidated, but instead the situation and the opposition inspired us. With five minutes to go, Cesc ran at the Milan defence and hit a twenty-yard shot past Zeljco Kalac and into the bottom corner of the net. Then, in the dying seconds, I got the ball on the right and headed for the byline. I felt like I was on a running track as I skipped past Massimo Oddo and crossed for Adebayor who was left with a tap-in. That finished the tie off completely and gave us a real boost. It was Milan's first defeat at home by English opposition. We had beaten the champions, and even though things had begun to go wrong in the Premier League, we knew we had a real shot at glory in Europe. We felt we could beat anybody left in the competition.

I would have preferred to avoid another English team in the quarter-finals because there's something more glamorous and different about testing yourself against players you don't come up against regularly in the Premier League. That didn't happen. We drew Liverpool.

We played the first leg at home. Adebayor put us a goal up midway through the first half but Dirk Kuyt equalized three minutes later. I came on after half-time when Van Persie picked up a thigh injury, and I thought I'd scored when I cut inside and shot from twenty yards but it went just wide. We should have had a penalty when Kuyt pulled back Hleb in the area but the referee waved play on. The game finished 1–1.

Despite what I said about preferring to face a foreign side, I was incredibly excited about playing a European match at Anfield. It was a special place for me to go because I had always been a Liverpool fan before I joined Arsenal. I didn't have any geographical connection with Merseyside or anything like that. I was a Liverpool fan because my dad was, although he's an Arsenal supporter now of course. When he was a kid he used to go round to his neighbour's house to play soldiers, and this neighbour supported Liverpool. That was enough for him, and I followed in his footsteps. The fact that Michael Owen played for them at the time cemented it all for me.

It was obvious we were going to have to play well to get through. The atmosphere at Anfield on big European nights like that is legendary. People who went to Liverpool's Champions League semi-final second leg with Chelsea in 2005 said it was a proper din. Some of the Chelsea players admitted afterwards that they had been taken aback by the volume of the noise. It had unsettled them. That night, when Luis Garcia scored his 'ghost goal', all the stuff Bill Shankly used to say about the Kop sucking the ball towards the net seemed to come true.

But, just like in Milan, we weren't intimidated by our surroundings or the opposition and we started stronger. I was on the bench again, desperate to be playing and nervous as anything because I couldn't affect what was happening on the pitch. Sitting on the bench is much more nerve-racking than playing because of that, and I was getting an awful lot of practice at it.

Some of the tension lifted when Diaby put us ahead in the first half. It sent optimism surging through us because we now had an away goal too. Sami Hyypiä equalized with a header for Liverpool and Fernando Torres put them ahead with twenty-two minutes left. That was a blow but it didn't really change things. We knew that if we got a second goal and stopped them scoring again, we would go through to the semis.

Four minutes after Torres scored, the Boss brought me on. I knew I could change things but I could see the clock ticking down on the digital read-out in the corner of the ground. It was on eighty-two minutes when Liverpool curled in a cross from the right, Steven Gerrard swung at it and missed, and it broke to me as I stood on the edge of the area. I took it past Xabi Alonso with my first touch, then past Fabio Aurelio with my second. I was shifting. The pitch opened up in front of me. On the commentary I heard later, Jim Beglin said that Aurelio should have brought me down, which is an interesting way of looking at it.

I was into the Liverpool half. Javier Mascherano was chasing me but he couldn't catch me and I knew I could keep going. I felt no one could touch me because I had got such momentum going. Hyypiä came out to meet me on the edge of the box and both he and Mascherano tried to tackle me at the same time but I jumped past them. I stumbled a bit and the touch took me too wide to shoot. I looked up and saw three Arsenal players unmarked in the box. I picked out Adebayor and he sidefooted it past José Reina from six yards out.

It was pandemonium. Adebayor wheeled away to celebrate on his own in front of the Arsenal fans at the Kemlyn Road end but the rest of the Arsenal players came to congratulate me. I was mobbed. And filled with euphoria. I thought I'd done something momentous. I thought I'd catapulted us into the semi-finals of the Champions League.

There was a bigger picture, too. In those seconds after that run, I felt like I had once and for all put the World Cup behind me. I felt like I had finally done something. Like I had proved that I was going to be a real player after all and that my career wasn't going to be downhill from Germany onwards. After all the things people had said about me after the World Cup, it showed that I was capable of special things. As I said, I was filled with utter euphoria.

It lasted about sixty seconds. That was the time it took for our young team to commit football's cardinal sin and lose concentration. We thought we were through to the last four and we switched off. Liverpool went straight back up to the Kop end, Ryan Babel surged into the box and Kolo Touré brought him down. Gerrard didn't swing and miss this time, he banged his penalty past Manuel Almunia and into the back of the net. If we scored again we could still go through, but as we poured everybody forward in stoppage time, Liverpool counter-attacked and Babel scored their fourth to put the tie out of reach.

I was shattered after the game. People were congratulating me about the run and commiserating with me about the result. I just couldn't shake the overwhelming sense of disappointment that we had got so close to the Champions League semis and the prize had been snatched away from us. If we had won at Liverpool, I don't think anyone would have stopped us. We would have gone to Moscow and we would have won the competition, not United. But that was our season all over. A tale of might-have-beens and what-ifs.

Five days later we lost 2–1 to United at Old Trafford which put them nine points clear of us at the top of the table with four games left to play. We won all of those games but it wasn't enough. I got our last goal of the season, in the 1–0 win at Sunderland on the final day, but, after having challenged for the title for so long, we finished third, behind United and Chelsea. Our eighty-three points would have been enough to win it in some seasons but not this one. United finished on eighty-seven points, Chelsea on eighty-five. I thought of all the things that might have been. What if we hadn't conceded that late goal at Birmingham and lost two points? What if we hadn't drawn with Wigan and Middlesbrough in the aftermath of the Birmingham game, both matches we should have won? We would have been champions.

Still, I felt like my career was just beginning. I felt like I'd cast off all the doubts that had surrounded me earlier in the season, all the suggestions about me moving away on loan, all the whispers that I wasn't going to make it. People were saying I was Arsenal's best player in the last few weeks of the season, and as far as I was concerned summer had come at the wrong time. I couldn't wait for the new season to start. I felt as though I'd turned a corner.

Thirteen

I was still only nineteen but I felt like I had become a regular for Arsenal. I'd played thirty-nine games in 2007–08 and scored seven goals. It began to dawn on me that I had made the transition from the wide-eyed boy who was so out of his depth in Germany to a real Premier League player. And with that status, whether I liked it or not, came a certain amount of exposure and fame.

Like I've said, I don't relish the limelight. I'm not a recluse or anything like that. I don't hide myself away. I don't hate being in the company of other people. I don't lock myself behind tinted windows and use VIP entrances to restaurants. But I'm not comfortable with people looking at me all the time when I'm walking down the street. Some footballers don't mind that. In fact, some make no bones about the fact that they enjoy it. In a way, I envy them that.

It comes with the territory of being a Premier League footballer these days. There's no getting away from that. If you play for a top club, you're a celebrity. You just have to get on with it. There are different ways of dealing with that. You can go to high-profile clubs and high-profile restaurants where paparazzi will be waiting outside or you can do what Paul Scholes did and keep yourself to yourself, rarely give interviews and lead a quiet family existence. But however you approach it, however low-key you try to be, people are going to want to know you and take pictures of you because of who you are. You have to accept that.

That year when I started playing regularly for Arsenal, I realized I was getting noticed a bit more on the street. I don't want to go out wearing sunglasses and a hat because that just draws more attention to yourself. But I do feel I have to be on my best behaviour all the time. I know I can't be rude to people, for instance. I'm always watching what I'm doing and making sure nothing I say can be mis-construed. I suppose I feel like I'm always on guard, always careful not to do the wrong thing.

Most people are incredibly polite. And I accept what people say about knowing that you're in trouble when people stop pestering you and asking for your autograph because when that happens you know you're not a successful player any more. I accept all that, and I accept that as an Arsenal player I have a certain responsibility to set the right example, especially towards kids who look up to professional footballers.

I'm just saying that occasionally the attention can be overwhelming. That's why I love going on holiday to New York. I can disappear there. Nobody knows who I am. Nobody cares who I am. I love the anonymity. It's a great city for that, a great place for melting into the background and watching people instead of them watching you. I'd like to live there one day, when my football career is over.

At home, it's the feeling of being watched that is strange. Once, I was in Debenhams and I could hear two women whispering about me. They were more like stage whispers, really, and I could hear everything they were saying. One of them was saying she was sure it was me and egging the other one on to ask me if I was Theo Walcott. Eventually one of them wandered over and did it and I said yes, I was indeed Theo Walcott.

'Give us a kiss,' she said.

I laughed that off and said I wasn't going to give her a kiss. I told her my girlfriend might be watching. I wasn't rude to her or anything. But she didn't like it.

She started saying that I was stuck up because I wouldn't kiss her and that I obviously thought I was too good for her and that footballers had become too big for their boots. It was all a bit bizarre.

I was beginning to get more attention from the media, too, and in the summer of 2008 Mel and I decided to do a photo shoot with *Hello!* magazine. I know that sounds a bit contradictory. I'm saying I don't like being recognized and I feel shy when people are looking at me and then there I am posing for photos with my girlfriend in a glossy magazine. Well, our logic for doing it was that we were receiving an increasing number of requests from people to do that kind of thing and we were also being followed on a fairly regular basis by paparazzi. There seemed to be a hunger to get pictures of Mel and me together, and we thought that if we did one organized shoot, that would help to calm it all down.

Mel and I felt the same about it. We'd been together for three years by then. We had a vague idea of how the celebrity world worked. Neither of us really wanted to embrace it but we didn't want to flee from it either. In fact, we both quite enjoyed the *Hello!* shoot. In contrast to looking over your shoulder to see where the paparazzi were, it was all quite relaxed.

Mel and I had met at the WestQuay shopping centre in Southampton in the summer of 2005. I was a scholar at Southampton at that time, right on the brink of making my first-team debut for the club, and feeling pretty pleased with myself. I was wandering through the shopping centre with a few of my mates, wearing my club tracksuit, when I spotted this girl standing outside the Claire's Accessories shop, holding a couple of wicker baskets with Claire's products in them.

I looked at her and I thought she looked at me. I walked up and down past the shop a couple of times. It wasn't very subtle. Neither was my next move. I mentioned to my mate Zach that I thought this girl was pretty good-looking. He said to me that the basket she was holding was for collecting boys' phone numbers. So I wrote mine on a piece of paper. Actually, I've got to be honest here and say I wrote my name on the paper too. My full name. I suppose I must have thought she might have heard of this kid who was going to do great things at Southampton. So I wrote Theo Walcott on this paper with my number and put it in Mel's basket.

She didn't have a clue who I was. But a couple of weeks later she rang me, and it went from there. We went to the cinema and watched two films in one night. *Dukes of Hazzard* was the second one, and the first was *Land of the Dead*, which was all about the living dead taking over the world. Very romantic.

It wasn't that scary but it did make Mel jump once or twice. We talked through most of it, which must have been a bit annoying for everyone who was trying to watch the movie, and we hit it off straight away. We had our first kiss after that film.

I made my first-team debut for Southampton at the beginning of August and things moved on with me and Mel. At the end of October I invited her to the home game against Stoke. I nearly screwed it all up by inviting another girl too, who was the sister of a friend of mine. She and Mel ended up practically sitting next to each other and Mel wasn't impressed. It wasn't the smartest move I ever made, but I just about survived.

We had only been going out for five or six months when I joined Arsenal. And then, when things went crazy when I got selected for the 2006 World Cup squad, Mel was catapulted into the limelight too. She dealt with it all really well. Probably better than me, actually. The paparazzi only upset her once. That was when one guy was particularly persistent when she was staying with my family in Baden-Baden during the tournament. She burst into tears that time, which seemed to be exactly what the photographer in question had been after all along. She was only seventeen and it was a lot of pressure all of a sudden to be facing that kind of attention.

She was labelled a Wag when she was in Germany but she didn't really become part of that circus. That was partly because she didn't know any of the other wives and girlfriends, but partly because, as I mentioned earlier, she wasn't staying at the same hotel as them and she couldn't afford to go shopping with them anyway. She got on with them fine when she was on the coach going to the games. She was the youngest of all of them but sometimes I think she felt she was the oldest.

Anyway, by the summer of 2008 we were both nineteen and we thought we might as well do a few things in public as a couple. We did the *Hello!* shoot and we also did an episode of *Celebrity Mr and Mrs*, the show that is supposed to test how well you and your partner know each other. We'd played the board game and we'd always done really well. In fact we always beat our friends, so when we were asked to do it we thought it would be a bit of fun.

We were on an episode with the former javelin champion Steve Backley and his wife Clare, and the Bee Gee Robin Gibb and his wife Dwina. It was a real laugh but we didn't do quite as well as we thought we would. When Philip Schofield and Fern Britton asked me whether I would be more scared of Arsène Wenger, my dad or Mel's dad, who had been the Mayor of Southampton the previous year, I picked

Arsène Wenger. When they took Mel out of the booth, where she'd had earphones and a blindfold on, she said she thought I'd have said my dad. My dad? Why would I be scared of my dad?

Then they asked me what I'd say if Mel said she'd been offered a million pounds to do a nude photo shoot for a magazine. Would I say categorically not, would I say it was up to her, or would I say she should go for it? I told them I'd say categorically not. I wouldn't want her to do that. No way. Mel wavered a little bit when they asked her. She almost said I would leave it up to her, but she picked the right answer in the end.

The last one they asked me was what Mel would say was the most romantic thing I had ever done. I told them I wasn't a romantic person. When they pressed me, I mentioned that I'd bought her a Beetle once and that it had been presented to Mel wrapped up in a ribbon. I had to admit that it was the car dealership that had come up with the idea of the ribbon, not me. So I went for that answer. Mel picked the time I'd given her a ring for Christmas. That hadn't occurred to me. Still, we got one out of three.

There was another round where we had to hold up a coloured paddle to signify which one of us we thought a statement identified best. If it was me, we had to hold up a blue paddle; if it was Mel, it was a pink paddle. So when they asked who had the most pairs of pants, I held up my blue paddle because I thought I had more than Mel, but she held up her pink paddle because she thought she had more than me. We didn't do too well on that round either. She said I screamed more on the rollercoaster at Thorpe Park and I said she screamed more. That was a misunderstanding really. I'm happy to admit I was more scared, but she screamed more. It was just that hers were happy screams and I was too nervous to open my mouth. They also asked us who had the prettier sister, Mel or me. Pretty dumb question, really, because Mel's always going to say her sister and I'm always going to say mine.

So we didn't win it, which annoyed us both a bit because we're both competitive, but we did OK. That was another one of the questions now I think of it: who's the most competitive? Each of us thought we were more competitive than the other. Actually, her competitiveness is one of the things I admire about Mel. I like the fact she's independent, too. She moved away from her family when she was eighteen to start a degree in physiotherapy at university in London and she's got a flat in south London. She divides her time between there and our place in Hertfordshire.

She's got no aspirations to become a full-time Wag. That doesn't do it for her. She wants to get on with her work. She doesn't want to be sitting at home waiting for me to come back from training. She wants to do something with her life. She wants to help people. She isn't really friendly with any of the England Wags. Not because she doesn't like them, it's just that she never really mixes with them. She's good mates with a couple of the partners of the Arsenal players. They have partners' nights out sometimes and she goes as often as she can, but sometimes her studies get in the way and she can't make it.

A few months before the 2010 World Cup, one of the papers ran a story about how Mel was embarrassed because I'd bought her a gunmetal-grey Ferrari California and she thought it was too flash for her to drive around in with her university mates. That made us both laugh. I bought it for her as a twenty-first birthday present and managed to keep it a surprise. When she walked into the garage and saw it parked there, she jumped up and down clapping her hands in that way that girls have. She certainly didn't look too embarrassed about it then.

Apart from other Arsenal players, we don't really hang out with any celebrities. Actually, there's one exception: the comedian Matt Lucas is a mate of ours. He's an Arsenal fan. He had a box at Arsenal and my dad got chatting to his brother, Howard, not knowing who he was. My dad will chat all night, and

Howard will too. They got friendly and started socializing, and I tagged along a few times and gradually got friendly with Howard and Matt, too. I went to Nobu in Berkeley Square with him recently and Mel and I went out with him and a friend to watch the *Alice in Wonderland* movie. I missed the Champions League semi-final between Inter and Barcelona on the TV that night but I was good. I didn't mention it once.

For my twenty-first birthday in March 2010, Mel organized a surprise for me, too. She arranged a big party at the Paramount Club at the top of Centrepoint, the skyscraper in London's West End. A lot of the Arsenal lads like Sol, Eduardo, Gaël and Andrei Arshavin came along and so did Matt Lucas and some of my old friends from Southampton like Gareth Bale and Jake Thomson. It was a great night. I don't often let myself go, but I did that night. We had just beaten Hull, we didn't have another match until the following Saturday, and, well, you're only twenty-one once. So, for once, I had a few drinks.

Mel had got the soul singer Beverley Knight along to sing and I disgraced myself by missing her singing Happy Birthday to me. I guess that's what happens when you have a few drinks. She was singing but I was in the toilets at the club giving an impromptu speech to my Arsenal teammates. I was making fun of

Andrei because he reminds me of one of the meerkats in those television ads, but mostly I was talking about them one by one and saying that no one could wish for a better set of teammates. The next day, everyone said I had made a very happy and good-natured drunk. That was good to know, though I'm not sure if Beverley Knight was too impressed.

Fourteen

I don't usually get involved in arguments. I avoid confrontation if I can. I don't feel the need to run forty yards during a game so I can jab my finger in someone's face. If a flare-up happens when I'm on the other side of the pitch, I tend to stay on the other side of the pitch. It's just not in my nature to seek aggravation. I prefer to let everything blow over rather than exacerbate the situation.

I'm not one of the more vocal members of the dressing room. Some of that is because I'm still learning as a player. It's a basic fact that most of my teammates, whether it's with Arsenal or England, are older than me. I suppose there's an element of natural deference in my character at the moment. I feel I should listen to more senior members of the team rather than shout out my own opinions. That includes our captain, Cesc Fabregas, obviously. Cesc is a bright bloke and he leads by example on the pitch. His never-ending effort, his drive and his determination make him an inspiring guy to play with but he also has fantastic vision, control and strength of character. He's the heart of the team and he deserves to be our leader.

I'm quite chilled out, basically. I let stuff flow over. I don't take much notice of people trying to wind me up. Physically it's hard to ignore someone if they kick you up in the air, but I don't react to that and I don't react to an opponent giving me verbals. I guess I've just got a fairly even temperament. I don't blame other people for snapping in the face of provocation, but I can usually stay level.

But there comes a time in everybody's career when you feel you have to stand up for yourself, a time when you think you're not a kid any more and that you don't just want to sit back and take it. For me, that moment came at half-time during one of the best matches I have ever played in, the 4–4 draw between Arsenal and Spurs at The Emirates at the end of October 2008.

Many of the details are in the public domain already, even if they were released in a form of code by William Gallas. Gallas was Arsenal captain at the time of that north London derby and a couple of weeks later he released his autobiography, *A Word for the Defence*. As usual with these things he did a few interviews to publicize the book, and in one of them he dropped some fairly heavy hints about what had gone on in the dressing room.

In the context of complaining about lack of respect from younger players for their elders in the modern game, Gallas said that not only was he shocked by the petulant attitude of some of the rising stars in the France squad but that he had had problems with members of the Arsenal team too. He mentioned the game against Spurs and how he had been insulted during the game by a player who was six years younger than him. Gallas said he had then had to intervene at half-time when the same player picked on another player in the dressing room and the pair nearly came to blows. The clues made it fairly obvious who the culprit was. Gallas was thirty-one and there were only three twenty-five-year-olds in the action against Spurs – Robin Van Persie, Emmanuel Eboué and Bacary Sagna – so everyone guessed immediately he was talking about Robin.

Actually, he was talking about Robin and me. I was the other person in the argument. I was the one Robin had taken issue with at half-time.

I had thought we were doing OK in the match, to be honest. Spurs were fired up because it was Harry

Redknapp's first game in charge and, after I had dragged a half-chance wide with a cross-shot, Spurs had taken the lead through a forty-yard volley from David Bentley. But we had more of the play and Mikael Silvestre equalized eight minutes before the interval.

When we got back into the dressing room at the break, Robin made it obvious he wasn't happy. And I was the reason he wasn't happy. I wasn't passing the ball enough, apparently. I wasn't being a team player, apparently. I was intent on being an individual, on playing only for myself, apparently. I didn't recognize the player he was shouting about as me. I thought I'd been doing OK.

It wasn't the first time he'd had a go at me. The same thing had happened during a pre-season tournament in Amsterdam in a game against Ajax. That time it was on the pitch, not in the dressing room. He accused me of wasting the ball and ignoring him when he thought I should have passed to him. He was pretty hyped up because he was on home soil and he wanted to put on a good show in front of his countrymen. He didn't like it when I ignored what he was saying.

'I am never ever going to pass you the ball again!' he yelled at me that time in Amsterdam.

'You're a big man then, aren't you?' I responded.

Robin wanted to fight me there and then, and it was the same in the dressing room at The Emirates during that game against Spurs. He was shouting at me and I wasn't having any of it. I wasn't going to take that from him. He kept going on about how I was just playing for myself, but I thought he was taking the easy option by trying to pick on one of the younger players and I told him he was out of order.

I stayed calm – I stayed sitting down – but he went absolutely nuts. I was trying to talk to him but he was past talking. There were people holding him back because he wanted to get at me. But I didn't back down. I wasn't a little kid any more. I think part of the reason Robin got so angry was that he was surprised I had answered him back in front of everyone else. I don't think he'd expected that.

Eventually, things calmed down. They had to, I suppose, because we were called out for the second half. The rest of the lads seemed a bit surprised things had flared up like that, but as soon as we got back out on the pitch the tension ebbed away.

Exchanges like that happen at football clubs all the time. They're bound to when people who are desperate to win are thrown together in high-pressure situations. It's just part of football.

There was no lingering resentment on my part and none on Robin's. In fact, early in the second half we combined to win a free-kick and Gallas scored from it to put us into the lead. The argument hadn't done any harm. It was the opposite, actually. When they're covered in the press, they're presented as rows laden with significance, but the reality is that they're over in an instant. You need those little tiffs now and again. If you don't get them, there is no passion in the team.

Every team needs someone who is very vocal like Robin, too. A lot of dressing rooms can be quiet these days, perhaps because there are so many players from different cultures crammed into them. But Robin is a good talker. He's a very intelligent man and he doesn't usually shout for no reason. In an ideal world you would only get encouragement from your teammates, but that probably wouldn't do a lot for your mental strength when things are stacked against you.

There's a danger that some people can shrivel if they get criticized by a teammate – it was often said that some of the Manchester United players were terrified of Roy Keane tearing into them when he was nearing the end of his career – but I always aim to bounce straight back from criticism like that. It doesn't have a lasting effect on me because I've got enough confidence in my ability to believe I can do the right thing on the football pitch.

There was a postscript to our argument, and I

don't mean the fact that Gallas was stripped of the captaincy soon after he had spoken about what had gone on. Later in the season, when we were playing Burnley in the FA Cup, Robin had another go at me during the game and started screaming about how I had chosen to shoot when he was better placed. I didn't react, but he went home that night and saw the game on television. When he came in the next day he admitted he had realized that actually he wasn't better placed than me after all. He apologized and said he had had no right to accuse me of being selfish. I was impressed that he did that. It takes a big man to apologize.

I'm sure we'll have more exchanges of views in the future but it doesn't bother me. I like Robin. He's a good character to have around. He's had his share of injuries, like me, and if we had had him around more I don't think we would have gone so long without winning a trophy.

But the period around that game against Spurs, as autumn moved into winter, was a difficult time for the club and for me. Arsenal had already suffered a couple of surprising defeats, away at Fulham and at home to Hull City, and the Spurs result knocked us back even further. We were 4–2 up with two minutes to go against Tottenham but then Jermaine Jenas and Aaron Lennon got late goals to rob us of victory.

When we got back to the dressing room, we felt as if we'd lost.

We'd had high expectations coming into the season. We'd only missed out on the title by a whisker the season before and we wanted to win it this time. We'd talked about our hopes on our pre-season tour of Austria. I'd set myself a target of having an injury-free pre-season and starting the first game of the Premier League campaign.

The method the Boss favoured for our meetings in Austria was to get us to split up into smaller groups and talk through what we wanted to achieve. Each group gets some ideas together and we put them up on the board. That's in front of the whole squad. My group was Adebayor, Robin, Nasri and Bendtner, the main attacking forces. (Later in the season, when we had a similar meeting in the Lowry Hotel in Manchester to revisit our resolutions, somebody left a copy behind and it got into the press.) I didn't do much talking in Austria. The vocal ones were Robin, Adebayor, Cesc, Kolo, Gaël Clichy and Nicklas. I'm a better listener. I am not ready to read out to the group yet. No way. I could do it, but it comes with seniority really.

Anyway, back then there was a genuine belief we could challenge United, Chelsea and Liverpool, so when the early season didn't go according to plan, it hit us hard. It was only the end of October but people had already written us off for the title and decided it was a straight race between Manchester United and Liverpool. A win against Spurs would have put us one point off the top of the table. But the question being asked about us most was not so much whether we had any chance of winning the league but whether we would make it into the top four at the end of the season and qualify for the Champions League.

In the aftermath of the Spurs result we lost three times in November, and even though we beat United and Chelsea, we began to slip out of contention for the league. Then, during an England training session in Berlin the night before we were due to play Germany, I suffered a fractured dislocation of my shoulder. It was a serious injury, and it put me out until March 2009.

That injury was a tough blow for me because when it happened I felt I was really beginning to establish myself as a first-team regular at Arsenal. At the start of the season I had been given the number 14 shirt that used to belong to Thierry Henry and I had begun to feel as though some of the magic of it was rubbing off.

I'd had two years wearing number 32 and I just felt I'd like a lower number, something that was symbolic of the fact I wasn't on the periphery any more. I asked for the number 8 actually, which was Freddie Ljungberg's old shirt, but Vic Akers, the kit manager, said that that had already been assigned to our only new signing of the season, Samir Nasri. I asked him what else was available. He said I could have 23, 19 or 14. Without thinking I said I'd take the 14 because it was the lowest. It didn't register immediately with me that that was Thierry's number. I took it, then suddenly I realized what I had done. A little bit of pressure came with wearing that number at our club. I didn't really want to call Vic back and tell him that I didn't feel up to wearing that number after all. So I just tried to convince myself that it was only a number. And then I made myself feel better by thinking that Thierry would probably be happy that I now had the 14 on my back. He had always been brilliant to me and I was proud to be wearing the shirt in which he had achieved so much. OK, so there was a lot to live up to, but it's good to set yourself the highest standards.

And things did start smoothly for me that season. I was playing well and my confidence was soaring. I scored my hat-trick for England against Croatia on 10 September and was hailed a hero on my return. When I played at Blackburn Rovers on the first weekend after the game in Zagreb, even the Blackburn fans at Ewood

Park applauded me every time I touched the ball. I was on cloud nine.

But a month later, when I injured my shoulder in Berlin, that season was in ruins. I was out for four months, and when I came back, Liverpool and United were neck and neck for the title and our hopes had gone.

It was a difficult campaign domestically. There's no point in denying that. One controversy seemed to follow hard on the heels of another. Gallas was stripped of the captaincy and there was constant speculation about the future of Emmanuel Adebayor. The Arsenal fans had never forgiven him for appearing to court a move to AC Milan in the close season, and sometimes the languid style of his performances fuelled their grievances. I didn't think he was a lazy player. Not particularly. I mean, he's a striker, and lots of strikers are lazy. Some people started calling him Offside Ade because he was caught out by the linesman's flag so often, but to me that was just a sign that he was always on the defender's shoulder. He scored some great goals for us, but by November 2008 there was a general air of dissatisfaction around The Emirates. The crowd was very quick to jump on us if we weren't playing particularly fluently. They even started to aim criticism at the Boss.

Gallas was stripped of the captaincy the week I

dislocated my shoulder in Berlin. He didn't travel with the team to the away game at Manchester City and it was a very tense and difficult time for the club. We lost 3–0 at Eastlands and the media said we were in crisis. Gallas was at the centre of the storm. I felt for William because he is a great professional and it was clear the whole thing had had a profound effect on him. He withdrew a little from the group around that time.

I never really had the feeling that the squad was divided between old and young. In the changing room, I suppose I sat in the young corner with players like Alex Song, Denilson, Aaron Ramsey, Robin and Gaël Clichy, but that didn't stop me respecting men like Pires, Sol Campbell, Ashley Cole, Dennis Bergkamp and Thierry Henry when I arrived. I respected them, and I respected William and Mikael Silvestre too. But the senior players need to respect the younger generation as well. We're all on the same side. We're all working towards the same target.

I get on fine with William. I always have done. He just wants to win. He has won so many trophies and he wanted to do it for Arsenal too. So he was very down when what he said about the conflicts within the Arsenal squad resulted in the captaincy being taken away from him and handed to Cesc. He would turn up for training and then go straight off afterwards. He sat in the corner alone, not talking to anyone, brooding. A lot of players didn't talk to him that much either. I don't really know why. He just seemed very miserable.

The thing is, in my opinion he was a great captain. Everyone talks about the Birmingham situation the season before, when he became overwrought when we conceded that late penalty, but he was a good leader. He was great at some of the off-field stuff too: organizing meetings and outings, go-karting, group trips to the O2 Arena and meals with the wives and girlfriends; what to do with money players were fined, which charities to give it to. He gave us a talk once about keeping the dressing room tidy and respecting the people who worked there. On the pitch he was always cajoling and encouraging and organizing. After we lost at home to Hull early in the season he arranged a meeting about it and said we had to move on. He was very good at lifting people's spirits.

Cesc Fabregas took to his new responsibilities well. He called a meeting about the dressing room too. A lot of the slips the players wear were being left in the showers, there was a lot of water in the changing room, and Cesc reminded everyone that Vic Akers had to clean it all up because we were being lazy. I guess respecting the dressing room is a bit of a theme at Arsenal. We have to appreciate how much other people do for us.

The nagging sense of dissatisfaction that was hovering over the club reached a low point at the start of December when we played Wigan Athletic at The Emirates. I was sitting up in my box with my family, recuperating after my shoulder operation, and that made it even more difficult to witness the way the Arsenal crowd turned on one of their own. All crowds can do it. We are all paid a lot of money in the Premier League now so the fans' expectations are, quite understandably, very high. The tolerance for someone having a bad day has gone. Still, I found it very uncomfortable to watch the way our supporters booed Emmanuel Eboué every time he touched the ball that afternoon. It was so bad that even though he had come on as a substitute for Samir Nasri after half an hour, the Boss felt the need to put him out of his misery and substitute Eboué himself right near the end. It was humiliating for him.

I felt embarrassed and angry for him, and, for the first and only time, ashamed of our fans. I accept absolutely that the supporters have paid their money and they have a right to boo if they want to. All I would question is quite what they were hoping to achieve by consistently jeering one of their own players. It isn't going to make him play any better, believe me.

We won the game 1–0, but when I left the stadium afterwards I didn't sign any autographs. Again, that's the first and only time that has happened. I know they may not have been the same people who were booing Eboué during the match but I just thought that what happened was awful. Emmanuel's a mate of mine. He's a decent lad. He's one of the jokers in the dressing room and I didn't like seeing him treated like that.

Sometimes, people get blinded by the thought of how much money players are earning and forget that other things might be quite difficult. Eboué's a guy from the Ivory Coast who is a long way from his friends and family. Later in the season he played in a game for his country against Malawi when a lot of fans were killed because a wall collapsed. It's not been easy for him.

It was wrong what happened to him, and it took me aback. It felt as though the fans had forced the manager into a decision. The day after the Wigan game, Emmanuel came into training and got on with it. Kolo Touré, who is also from the Ivory Coast, had a quiet chat with him about it but everyone else wanted to let him forget about it. He's the last person that should have happened to. He was just made into a scapegoat because the season wasn't going quite as everyone had hoped.

That kind of thing seemed to happen a lot that season. Gabriel Agbonlahor went through a barren spell in front of goal and the Aston Villa fans started booing him. I couldn't believe that. I mean, he was only twenty-one and he had scored so many goals. Then there was Ashley Cole being jeered at Wembley because he made a mistake against Kazakhstan. He underhit a backpass, that was all, and suddenly everyone was on his back. It wasn't like he meant to do it. I was sitting on the bench that day, and to hear an England player being victimized by his own supporters at Wembley was odd and very uncomfortable.

I don't know what I'd do if I got booed by my own fans. It would be very unsettling, I know that. Being jeered by the opposition is totally different. I know some players who actively like that because it shows that the other team's supporters have singled you out as someone to fear. After my run against Liverpool in the Champions League quarter-final at Anfield, I got the ball again in midfield and I heard a collective intake of breath from the Liverpool fans because they were worried about what was coming next. That made me feel good.

I only really get booed on a regular basis at Portsmouth, and that's because of my association with Southampton. When we played at Fratton Park

Old Trafford, 30 May 2006. Sitting on the bench (**left**) wondering if I'd get on for my international debut against Hungary and then (**below**) coming on for Michael Owen midway through the second half. At seventeen years and seventy-five days, I became the youngest player ever to play for England.

One week later I was getting on the team bus in Baden-Baden, but it proved to be a frustrating summer.

Above: In October 2006, I was back in Germany with the Under-21s. This time I showed what I could do when I scored both goals in a 2–0 win in Leverkusen.

Below: The Germans got their revenge in the 2009 European Championship final. Getting a runners-up medal is never a great feeling, and that summer in Sweden was another learning experience.

Below: David Beckham – what can you say? He's been great with me and always has time for a chat and word of advice.

Right: I broke another record on 10 September 2008 when I became the youngest player to score a hat-trick for England. Here Rio Ferdinand congratulates me for my first goal against Croatia.

My third goal (**above**) came after a brilliant defence-splitting pass from Wayne Rooney. My celebration (**below**) still needed some work, though!

Above left and right: Coming on for Freddie Ljungberg to make my Arsenal debut, against Aston Villa. I watched and studied DVDs of Freddie's runs to help improve my game. 19 August 2006 will always be another treasured day in my memory.

My first experience of a north London derby came in the semi-finals of the Carling Cup. It was a tough battle at White Hart Lane, as you can see here, with Benoit Assou-Ekotto and Anthony Gardner double-teaming me.

Above and left: The 2007 Carling Cup final at the Millennium Stadium in Cardiff got off to the best possible start when I curled the ball past Petr Cech for my first Arsenal goal. I went a bit crazy with my celebrations!

Unfortunately two goals by Didier Drogba were enough for a full-strength Chelsea team to beat our young Arsenal side. Cesc Fabregas (**left**) and Thierry Henry (**right**) offer me some consolation for the defeat.

Left: The Champions League has provided some great nights at the Emirates. My first goals in the competition came against Slavia Prague in October 2007.

Below: The atmosphere at Anfield is incredible, too, on European nights. After going past half the Liverpool team including Xabi Alonso here, I thought I'd put us in the semi-finals, but it wasn't to be.

Below: I was fired up when I came off the bench to score against Barcelona in our Champions League quarter-final in March 2010. The fans went nuts too!

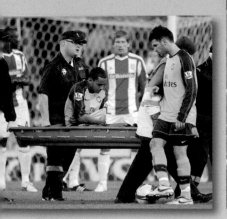

Injuries are part of the game. At least my shoulder problems seem to be behind me now.

Stretchered off in Switzerland in September 2010. I had started the season in great form, so this was extra frustrating.

Left and below: An ankle sprain against Stoke later that season gave our physio Colin Lewin more work. It saw me miss the Carling Cup final against Birmingham, as well as another agonizing loss to Barcelona.

Above: My first Premier League goal came against Birmingham in February 2008, but the day was overshadowed by the horrific injury to Eduardo.

Above: The 2010–11 season was my most prolific so far, including my first Arsenal hat-trick against Blackpool in August. It was also a breakthrough year for Jack Wilshere, but how we could have done with Thomas Vermaelen not being injured.

Right: My thirteenth goal of the campaign came at Fulham on the final weekend, with Robin Van Persie also on the scoresheet. Here's to lots more in the future!

towards the end of the 2008–09 season, though, one Pompey fan tried to take things a step further.

When I was warming up before the game, their fans were singing the usual stuff about me being a Scummer, which is their nickname for anyone connected with Southampton, and that was it. But it was a warm day and I'd been drinking from a water bottle just before kick-off. Before the game began, I put it on a ledge next to our dug-out so that I could get to it easily when there was a break in play and top up with liquids. But during the match, my dad, who was up in the stands, phoned Paul Irwin, Arsenal's player liaison manager, and said he needed to get a message to the bench urgently. He had seen a Portsmouth fan grab my water bottle, without anybody noticing, unscrew the cap, spit into it six or seven times, then screw the cap back on. The message got through just as someone went down injured and I was heading over to take a drink. They had time to warn me, but what if the message had come through a couple of minutes later? That's a nice thought. I don't mind the Scummer stuff, but the water bottle thing is really not very pleasant. I was getting racial abuse from some bloke in one of the sponsors' boxes too. Fratton Park is not on my list of favourite places to visit.

Fifteen

I finally made my return to first-team action on 8 March in an FA Cup fifth-round tie at home to Burnley. The medical staff at Arsenal had been superb. Tony Colbert, Neal Reynolds, Colin Lewin, all the masseurs – everyone was just brilliant. They had been so encouraging and supportive, and I wanted to pay them back on the pitch. I was really grateful for everything they did. At times, when my morale might have dipped and it seemed like a long road back to fitness, Neal really kept me going.

The landscape of that 2008–09 season when I returned was rather different to the way it had been when I was injured back in November. Even though we were on a decent unbeaten run, we were out of contention for the league and Fabregas was the skipper, not Gallas. But we were still in the

Champions League. The first leg of our second-round tie against Roma had come just too early for me, but I was fit for the second leg and named among the substitutes.

We were a goal up from the first leg at The Emirates but Roma wiped that out after nine minutes at the Stadio Olimpico when Juan put them level on aggregate. I feared the worst when they got that early goal because it put pressure on us straight away. They had quite a lot of chances as well. Francesco Totti went close a few times and they had a big shout for a penalty turned down just before half-time.

I knew I was going to come on at some stage. During the game I was thinking, 'I hope this doesn't go to penalties.' I shouldn't have been thinking about that. I should have been concentrating on the game. But I just had a feeling about it because even though Roma had their chances, no one was really on top. I came on fifteen minutes from the end of normal time but, sure enough, the aggregate score was still level at the end of extra time.

The Boss had already drawn up his list of who he wanted to take the kicks and in what order. When we were practising pens in training I'd been pretty shocking, but the Boss came up to me and said I was going third. By then I'd asked Denilson, who already knew he was going to be fifth, whether I could swap with him because I wanted to take the one that might be the winner. When the Boss said I was down at number three I asked him if I could go to four or five, but I don't think he heard me so I stayed at three. I was pleased he had the faith in me to stick me in among the takers but I was nervous all the same.

Eduardo took our first kick but it was saved by Alexander Doni. They scored their first, then Van Persie scored our second, then Mirko Vucinic hit one of the most feeble penalties I'd ever seen, a kind of tapped chip that barely got off the ground and was easily saved by Almunia. That felt like a real gift. Our spirits lifted.

So the scores were level when it came to my turn. The walk to the spot felt like an absolute mile. My whole throat went dry. Everything was in slow motion. I kept thinking about James Beattie, back in the day with Southampton. He was the best penalty taker I've ever seen. He used to put the ball down, walk back, turn round, not even look at the goal-keeper, run up, whack it and score. I thought I'd take that attitude into my penalty.

I didn't change my mind about where to put the ball, something experienced penalty takers always say is fatal. I'd decided to try and hit it low and hard to the keeper's right and I stuck with that. It didn't quite work out as I'd hoped, though. It was a bit too closc to Doni and he almost saved it. I mean, he really nearly saved it. I thought for a split second that he'd kept it out and my heart nearly leapt out of my throat, but as he tried to push the ball away it squirmed under his body and crept into the corner of the net. I tried not to look as if I had been on the verge of having a nervous breakdown but all I could think when I looked up at the fans was 'Thank God'.

Former Arsenal player Julio Baptista scored for them, Nasri scored for us, Vincenzo Montella scored for them and now it was sudden death. Back in the centre circle I could hardly breathe. Denilson hit his penalty straight down the middle, Totti levelled it at 4–4, Kolo Touré put us back ahead, Alberto Aquilani, who moved to Liverpool at the start of the following season, put them back on level terms. Bacary Sagna scored for us. Surely this time they would crack. But no, John Arne Riise buried his kick too.

I was starting to get worried. I looked over at Gallas, who was down as our last penalty taker, and he didn't look good. If it had come down to him taking a penalty, I wouldn't have been too confident. But it didn't come to that. We didn't need William in the end. Abou Diaby took our eighth penalty and put us back ahead, and finally, finally, finally, Max Tonetto blasted his shot high over the bar.

We all ran to Almunia and swamped him. It felt like a big night for us. It was a young team we'd fielded: Sagna, Eboué, Denilson, Bendtner, Diaby, Nasri and me, coming off the bench. I suppose, because I broke through when I was young, my career has been filled with events that have felt like a coming of age. This was certainly another one. We had won without Cesc as well. It felt as if those of us who had gone through it would come out of it richer for the experience.

And that experience in the Stadio Olimpico had one other lasting effect on me. Until I played in that tie I used to watch cup matches on the television and hope they went to penalties. I wanted to see the drama. Rome was my first experience of actually being involved in the drama. And it was horrible. Now, whenever I see a game, I think, 'Don't go to penalties,' because I know exactly what the players will be going through.

The result in Rome gave our season a huge fillip. We were out of contention for the Premier League title by then, down to fifth place in the table, but now we had more Champions League ties to look forward to and an FA Cup quarter-final against Hull City. It was a bit of a grudge match for us because Hull had produced one of the shock results of the season when they won at The Emirates in September. That was part of a tremendous run they went on before Christmas, but their progress had stalled in the second half of the season and they were now plummeting towards the relegation zone. There was a feverish desperation about them when they came back to The Emirates that night in March.

They took an early lead through Nick Barmby and then set about frustrating us with niggly fouls and time-wasting. Things began to get a bit heated on the touchline, and the Hull assistant manager, Brian Horton, was getting really excitable. I've never seen anything like it. When the half-time whistle went and I was walking towards the tunnel, I could hear him yelling at the Boss. He was really stressed. Some of the other lads said Horton had been eyeballing our bench all through the first half. It was bizarre. I guess it was the pressure of their situation.

The Boss stayed as calm as you like. 'Come and see me in my office after the game if you have something you would like to discuss,' he said to him.

It was the same in the second half. Horton hadn't calmed down at all, he just kept on raving, and it got to the point where some of our players found his antics pretty comical.

We put them under a lot of pressure and Robin equalized fifteen minutes from the end. Gallas got the winner ten minutes later, and, inevitably, there was an element of controversy about it. Hull claimed Gallas was offside when he scored and they went nuts.

As I said, the atmosphere between the two benches was already very tense. Gaël Clichy was still seeing the funny side of it. He wasn't involved in the game but he was down on the touchline and he kept holding up two fingers on one hand and one on the other to Horton to remind him what the score was. That didn't really calm him down much. When the final whistle went, Horton looked to me like his head was going to explode.

I had been substituted when the scores were level but I went out on to the pitch at the end to celebrate with the rest of the lads. That's when it all started to get really unpleasant. Cesc was injured at the time but he had been watching from the stands and he strolled on to the pitch in his jeans and Puffa jacket, which had a hood, to acknowledge the fans and congratulate the players. At one point he spat on the ground, which players often do after a match. Horton claimed that Cesc had spat on him, which wasn't the case. The row over that went on and on and it was a couple of months later when an independent FA commission cleared Cesc.

That did nothing to soothe people's emotions on the night, of course. When I got back to the players' tunnel, all I could see was a mass of people shouting and shoving and swearing and flailing. It was like a scene from that film *300*. There was an army of stewards separating our dressing room from their dressing room. The Hull players were trying to climb over the stewards to get to our players. It was absolute pandemonium.

Brian Horton was there still. At the time I didn't have a clue that he thought Cesc had spat at him. I know Cesc would never have spat on someone. He's the captain of Arsenal Football Club. He has a keen sense of the responsibility he carries. He wouldn't do that. A bit later, the Hull manager, Phil Brown, started going on about the fact that Cesc had been wearing a 'hoody', as though that automatically made him some kind of thug. That made Brown sound like a schoolgirl to me. It's not the clothes, it's the person.

The stuff in the tunnel was all handbags really. I couldn't see any punches. A few of our players were there, just watching, and eventually the stewards calmed it down. I'm the sort of person who when there's a fight going on will just sit down on the floor and watch. I don't want to get involved in all that. But I don't think it necessarily reflects badly on people. It just shows how much passion players have within them for the game. I wish the fans could see that sometimes when there is all this talk about how players don't have passion for the game any more.

If a player doesn't have passion, he won't go anywhere in the game. He'll disappear. If a player doesn't have passion, he won't be able to fight back from adversity. Collectively, we had shown our passion in Rome and against Hull. Suddenly, our season was on fire again, full of possibilities.

Sixteen

The climax to the 2008–09 campaign didn't go well. Actually, it turned into an anti-climax. We beat Villarreal in the quarter-finals of the Champions League, overshadowing the return of the old maestro Robert Pires with a performance that showed that even though we were young, we were feeling invincible. But then we lost to Manchester United in the semis. We lost to Chelsea in the semi-finals of the FA Cup too, and there was another round of soul-searching from our fans, who were as disappointed as we were about the way our campaign had been extinguished.

It's at times like that that you realize what an inspirational man Arsène Wenger is. When other leading clubs have big setbacks, they sometimes seem to find it hard to recover from them. It often leads to radical changes. Either the manager goes or there are sweeping changes in personnel or there is a significant shift in the philosophy of the club, usually a move away from youth to the safety of experience. But because of the Boss, we ride those setbacks at Arsenal much better. There is always optimism about the future. Some people say it's a 'jam tomorrow' culture and that tomorrow never comes. But it doesn't feel like that when you're part of it. Even when our season fell apart in the spring of 2009, it still felt as if there was a bigger picture. It felt as if we were building towards something and that our progress had been interrupted, not halted. My faith in him has never been shaken.

That feeling of progress and optimism centred round the Boss was one of the main reasons why I signed a new contract at Arsenal two weeks before the end of the season. There had been a lot of talk about the fact that Real Madrid were desperate to sign him as their manager so that he could oversee the new *galáctico* project that had brought Kaká, Xabi Alonso, Karim Benzema and Cristiano Ronaldo to the Bernabéu, but once again the Boss showed his loyalty to Arsenal and turned Madrid down.

I was worried about it for a while, though. The Boss went to a question-and-answer session with Arsenal shareholders at The Emirates about the time

I signed my new deal and had a few fierce exchanges with disgruntled fans. He was particularly critical of supporters who jeered at the players during home games. Someone said that it sometimes seemed like we weren't trying, and he took exception to that. He talked a lot about the 'negative environment' The Emirates can sometimes become if things are not going well for us. He also told the meeting that there was no point 'slaughtering' players unless the crowd wanted to destroy their confidence. He's absolutely right about that. Later in the meeting someone branded Mikael Silvestre 'a geriatric' and the Boss snapped back at him, 'I cannot accept that you speak about the players of your club like that. You are attacking the players, and that is much worse than attacking me.'

At the same meeting he defended Emmanuel Adebayor, too. Adebayor had become the focus of a lot of fans' frustration all season and there were a couple of games where he didn't do himself any favours. But he did score a magnificent goal with an overhead kick in the first leg of the Champions League quarter-final against Villarreal after we had gone a goal down.

I thought Adebayor was a fantastic player, but I have to be honest and admit that very occasionally his attitude let him down. There was the odd game where he seemed to get caught offside over and over again to the point where it became carelessness. I was also surprised, after we had been knocked out of the Champions League by United in a comprehensive home defeat in the semi-final second leg, to look across the dressing room and see him laughing and joking with a few people while the rest of us were trying to come to terms with the crushing disappointment of what had just happened. But that was Addy.

I suppose I shouldn't have been surprised when the next season, after he had joined Manchester City, he ran the length of the pitch at Eastlands to celebrate in front of the Arsenal fans after he had scored for his new club. Later in the game he stamped on Robin Van Persie's head. He said afterwards that he was upset because some of the Arsenal players wouldn't shake his hand before the game. I don't know if that happened. I wasn't there. But nothing could justify what he did to Robin, nor his show of disrespect to the supporters, even if he did apologize later.

The Boss even had to defend me at one point during the meeting. One shareholder asked if he was confident that players like me, Alex Song and Abou Diaby were good enough to play in a team that was capable of winning the title. The Boss pointed out that if Arsenal decided they wanted to let any one of the three of us leave, the club would be inundated with offers. 'They are great players, and they will show you they are great players,' he said.

Everyone appreciates support like that from their manager. It means an awful lot. I don't feel that I've had a rough ride from the Arsenal crowd. In fact they've always treated me fantastically. I also know there are bound to be a few fans in any group of football supporters who want to have a go. It's unrealistic to think everyone's going to be cheering you every minute of every match. You have to be strong enough to ignore some voices. Still, it was good of the Boss to leap to my defence.

The fact that the Boss stayed at Arsenal when Real Madrid came in for him was massive for me. The way he developed players like Thierry Henry, the way he nurtured them, impressed me so much. I want him to develop me into a striker the same way he did with Thierry. I signed a new contract because of him and the belief I have got in the team's ability to win major honours.

I just can't imagine the Boss anywhere else. It wouldn't look right him sitting on the home bench at the Nou Camp or the Allianz Arena, and I can't see him doing it. From Arsenal's point of view, it would be incredibly hard for someone to come in and replace him, even harder than the job of following Sir Alex Ferguson at United. They are both men who have put their stamp on their clubs and given them something more than just trophies. They've imposed a philosophy on their clubs, too, and they're both committed to attacking, attractive football. But I still think the Boss would be the harder man to follow. Arsenal's entire identity is wrapped up with him now and with his methods. He is involved in every aspect of running the club. Arsenal is in the Boss's blood now and I would be devastated if he left.

The players don't actually see him that much after a game. If we have lost, we don't see him in the dressing room. He doesn't come straight in. He's not the sort of character to sit everyone down and have a go at them. It's more his style to have a meeting a couple of days later so we can do a proper, rational analysis of what happened. If you've lost, there's no point having a go at your players because they're already at a low ebb anyway.

The Boss isn't a teacup thrower at half-time either. Nothing like that. Usually it will be very quiet for ten minutes and then he will say what has to be said. The message comes across. When he speaks, everyone listens. He commands the instant respect of all the players. If we are not playing well, he will point out the good things we are doing. He will talk in a positive way. He always speaks in English if it's a general message, but if he pulls one of the

French-speaking lads aside, he speaks in French.

Another reason he commands respect is that he is straight with the players. He keeps faith with the group. He has talked a lot over the last couple of years about his confidence in the young players at the club and why one of the reasons he is wary of going out and spending a lot of money on established stars is that he does not want to impede the progress of the younger players as they reach maturity.

I didn't sit down face to face with the Boss during the negotiations for my new contract. When it had got to the stage where we only needed to finalize small details he approached me for a chat and gave me an idea of where he thought I was in my development. He said he didn't think I was at Wayne Rooney's level but that I would get there. He said he'd gradually move me into a position as a central striker over the next couple of years, which was what I wanted to hear. No one has seen me up front yet, not really, but I still think of that as my best position. In my first couple of seasons at the club, though, we haven't really had a dedicated right-winger so I can understand why I've been asked to play there.

The other thing that was music to my ears was that the Boss said he wanted to work with me for the next couple of years, which was even more evidence that his long-term future is at the club. That means a lot to all of us at the club. I look at the players who have worked under him and see how well they are doing and I want to continue to be a part of that. I also look at players who left when maybe they should have stayed, people like Mathieu Flamini and Alexander Hleb, who seem to be struggling without the Boss's influence. Their careers seem to me to have taken a backward step.

If there's one player I think even the Boss might regret letting go, it's probably Lassana Diarra. I have never seen such a hard-working centre midfielder as him. He was so small but so strong. Unbelievably good. But at the time he was at Arsenal he was behind Flamini and Fabregas in the pecking order and he didn't have the patience to stick it out. He wanted first-team football and he wanted it now. If he had stayed just a little longer he would have been straight into the side once Flamini left for AC Milan, but by then he had moved on to Portsmouth and then Real Madrid.

Diarra didn't look at the long-term with Arsenal. I make sure I never forget that the Boss has my long-term interests at heart. I have already come across managers who appear to think about their own futures before they think about a player's welfare. I know of one manager who played young players who were struggling badly with injuries because he was under pressure in his job. One of those players has had long-term injury problems since then. To my mind it's because he was overplayed when he should have been rested.

So even though I don't like being rested and I don't like being substituted, deep down I know it's for the best when the Boss makes the decisions he makes. I trust his judgement. He did it in April 2009 when we played against Wigan in the league game that was sandwiched between the two legs of the Champions League quarter-finals against Villarreal. The Boss switched me to play up front at half-time and I got our equalizer after an hour. Then he took me off a few minutes later. When I asked him about it, he laughed and said he had taken me off because I was playing so well. Then he explained that he wanted to save me for the second leg of the Villarreal tie. The thing is, he has seen so many young players burn out and start to pick up niggling injuries that hamper their careers. One of the promises he made to my parents and to Warwick when I signed for Arsenal was that he wouldn't let that happen to me. He couldn't protect me against injuries I might sustain from tackles, but he was adamant that when I reached physical maturity at twenty-one I would not have been overplayed.

I've seen it. I know it happens. People have

mentioned the example of Norman Whiteside to me as another player who burst on to the scene very young. He had a great career with Manchester United and Northern Ireland but he started to pick up injury after injury and had to retire at the age of twenty-six after a succession of knee problems. I don't want that to happen to me.

So even though there have been times when I've been upset after being taken off, even though I have felt the need in the past to speak to him about not getting a regular first-team spot, I have never really doubted the Boss. He's a good communicator. You're never left wondering why something has happened to you. Or why it isn't happening.

He's always keen to do what's best for a player but he is not afraid of being ruthless either. When we lost to a late Didier Drogba goal against Chelsea in the FA Cup semi-final at Wembley he was angry because our goalkeeper Lukasz Fabianski hadn't given away a penalty when Drogba went round him. Lukasz had come rushing out of his area to try to thwart Drogba but Drogba had sidestepped him relatively easily and Lukasz didn't really commit to the challenge. The Boss said that sometimes you have to make personal sacrifices to win trophies and that we had failed to do it.

Maybe that goes against the common idea of the

Boss as the great idealist of the game. I think he is an idealist, but he is also wise enough to know that sometimes you have to do what needs to be done if you are going to win. I'd put us ahead in that match in the first half and we had a great chance of going through to the final but we lost it on mistakes. As a team, we need to be a bit more clever sometimes. Other teams do it.

The Boss surprised a few people the next season as well, in January 2010, after a game against Everton at The Emirates. Some time in the second half Denilson was running with the ball in midfield when he suddenly keeled over, clutching his side. The ball ran loose and Everton nearly scored. After the game, the boss told Denilson that if that ever happened again he wanted him to make sure he handled the ball as he fell as that way the game would have to be stopped while he was treated. There was a bit of comment about that the next day and some headlines suggested the Boss was advocating cheating. He wasn't. He just wanted us to become a little more streetwise.

I know what he means, and I think I know where to draw the line when it comes to gamesmanship. In the second leg of the quarter-final against Villarreal at The Emirates in April 2009, a few days before that FA Cup semi-final against Chelsea, I won a penalty that wasn't a penalty. I'd already scored our first goal by lifting the ball over the keeper when he came rushing out to meet me after a neat flick through by Cesc. That put us ahead on aggregate and then Adebayor got a second. About ten minutes after Adebayor's goal I got to the byline and went to do a Cruyff turn instead of crossing it. A Villarreal defender, Diego Godin, came sliding in for a tackle and got the ball. But he took me out in the process. My instinct was that it wasn't a penalty, but the referee gave it. The Villarreal players were incensed and surrounded me and accused me of cheating. One of them, Sebastian Eguren, protested so much he was sent off. But what could I do? The referee had made his decision. It wasn't up to me to challenge it.

Something similar happened in our league game at Portsmouth a few weeks later. It was a big game for us because we knew we would be guaranteed a place in the top four if we won. We had gone a goal up early in the game, and then a few minutes before half-time Andrei Arshavin was brought down in the box by Sean Davis and the referee awarded a penalty. Andrei got up and started wagging his finger at the ref as if to say it wasn't a foul, but I grabbed him and pulled him away. I told him the referee had already given it and that we could do with a 2–0 lead at half-time to give us some breathing space. There's nothing you can do in that situation. If you're through on goal and you dive, that's different. You've deliberately cheated. But if the ref gives it, that's it. There are plenty that go against you so you have to take the ones that go for you.

I again saw the ruthless side of the Boss in the second leg of our Champions League semi-final against United at The Emirates. We were a goal down from the first leg at Old Trafford and we desperately needed a good start to get back into the tie. We were fired up and the crowd was brilliant. The Boss had made a point of urging them to get right behind the team and be raucous for that night especially, and they responded magnificently. There was a brilliant atmosphere inside The Emirates when the game kicked off.

But after eight minutes, Cristiano Ronaldo broke down the left and hit a first-time cross towards the back post. Kieran Gibbs, our young left-back, who was standing in for Gaël Clichy, was about to cut the cross out when he slipped on the turf. The ball went straight to Ji-Sung Park, who scuffed a shot over Almunia and into the back of the net.

Kieran was distraught. He put his hands on his head. He tried to retrieve the ball as quickly as possible so we could get on with the restart. Robin Van Persie went over to him to try to encourage him.

But we all knew in that moment that we now needed to score three goals to overhaul United on aggregate and that it was a mountain to climb. When Ronaldo beat Almunia with a long-range free-kick three minutes later, the tie was effectively over.

I felt for Kieran. He's a very good young player with a bright future ahead of him. What happened against United was just bad luck. He seemed to make a decent enough recovery but Ronaldo was just in one of those moods in the first half. He was practically unplayable. At that time he was the best player in the world. Better than Messi, I thought. More dominant. They're different, obviously, but Ronaldo can be a target man as well as a winger. He's good in the air. He's got everything. And he was doing it in the Premier League, which is the best there is. I didn't see much of Messi in the other semi-final between Barcelona and Chelsea. I thought that summed up the difference between them at the time.

So, all in all, it was a pretty tough forty-five minutes for Kieran. When we got into the dressing room at half-time, the Boss said he was taking him off and replacing him with Eboué. As soon as he said it I looked at Kieran and saw his face fall. He slumped. I have never seen that happen to someone before. The next thing, he was up and gone into the showers. He was really upset. I suppose the last chance he had of trying to put things right had been taken away. I went to put an arm round him after the game. It was a hard setback for him to take.

I hadn't really played that well myself over the two legs of the semi-final. We had been outplayed at Old Trafford. We were lucky to come away with only a one-goal deficit, which was a credit to Almunia, who pulled off some world-class saves. I was quiet for most of that match. I found it difficult to get into the game. We didn't really create that much. We kept the ball OK but we lacked aggression in the final third.

It was quite difficult that night because we were playing with just one up front. That meant Patrice Evra, who's the toughest left-back I've ever played against, mainly because of his relentless work rate up and down the pitch, didn't have to worry about a second forward and had licence to attack. They already had two versus one at the back so he could push on. That meant I had to come back and defend instead of him worrying about me getting in behind him. I couldn't leave Sagna, our right-back, to defend against Evra and Wayne Rooney. I wasn't really happy about my performance in the final third but there was hardly any chance of me getting forward because Evra was pushing me back all the time. When I was spinning in behind, there was no space. It was a hard night, but after that first-leg match the Boss kept on saying we had to believe in what we could do. I thought we could win 1–0 at The Emirates and take it to extra time. But it didn't work out like that.

Evra said afterwards that the match had felt to him as if it was men against babies and that United, Barça and Chelsea were in a different class to Arsenal. That kind of thing can come back to haunt you. Sadly for him, Barcelona versus United in the final looked like men against babies too. Mind you, Evra was right that they had too much experience for us. Over the two legs, it was clear that they were the better team. But the biggest players shouldn't be disrespectful like that. They know that in football, fortunes can change.

Anyway, I thought we had a lot to be proud of that season. Reaching the semi-finals of the Champions League for the second time in the club's history and the semi-finals of the FA Cup isn't too bad. It's not what we wanted but it still showed we were among the elite and getting very close to winning the trophies we so desperately want to bring back to The Emirates for our fans.

There were other achievements, too. More subtle achievements. Stepping stones, I suppose. Coming through the penalty shoot-out against Roma. Beating Fenerbahçe 5–2 at the Sukru Saracoglu Stadium in Istanbul in the Champions League group phase. That was a great experience because I had never played in Turkey before and the atmosphere at grounds there is like nowhere else. I could see our fans singing at the start of the game but I couldn't hear them because the Fenerbahçe supporters were making such a racket. They were letting off fireworks and flares and bouncing up and down. I had never seen anything like it. And we didn't even get the full treatment. They clapped us off at the end because we had played so well.

I played against Roberto Carlos that night. I was nervous when I found out because I presumed he'd be attacking all night, haring down their left-hand side like he always used to. He's one of the legends of our game, but he was coming to the end of his career by then and in the match it was obvious he had lost a lot of his discipline. He didn't really stay in position. He left too much of a gap between the centre-back and him, and Cesc played a ball in for me in that position and I went round the keeper and scored our second goal.

Then there was our match at Liverpool a week before the first leg of the Champions League semi-final with United. Liverpool still had an outside chance of winning the Premier League at that time and a lot of people thought that we would put out a weakened side. That, they argued, would give us the double benefit of resting players for the Champions League and handing Liverpool a win that would bring them closer to United and make it impossible for United to rest players in the league game before the semi-final with us.

It was a decent conspiracy theory, but I don't think it ever crossed the Boss's mind.

We took a strong side up there and fought out one of the epic matches of the season, a 4–4 draw that swung one way and then the other. Anyone who didn't know the league positions and was trying to pick which side was still desperately fighting for the title would never have guessed it wasn't us.

There was no hint of it being a second-class game for us in any way. At that stage we weren't absolutely stitched on ahead of Aston Villa for fourth place but we could have afforded to take it a little easy if that had been part of our mentality. It wasn't. We were fantastic going forward, and when I came on for Denilson with twenty-five minutes to go it had already developed into a rip-roaring game.

None of the Liverpool fans gave me any stick when I ran on. Maybe they remembered what had happened the last time I came on as a substitute at Anfield. I got the same thrill running on as I'd had that night I went on my run in the Champions League quarter-final the season before.

We were 2–1 down when I came on and within a couple of minutes Arshavin, who had got our first, had equalized. Andrei got his hat-trick three minutes later to put us ahead, and two minutes after that Torres equalized to make it 3–3. It was breathless stuff and we were still level going into injury time. Then a corner we were defending was headed out and I got to it just before Yossi Benayoun and set off. It was a déjà vu moment, but as I sprinted towards their goal I saw a small figure hurtling into view out of the corner of my eye. Andrei had put his head down and kept up with me. The ball got stuck between my feet but I dug it out and rolled it across to him. He still had a lot to do but he smashed it in.

He's some player, Arshavin. I make fun of him sometimes because he bears a passing resemblance to Alexsandr the meerkat in the television advert. I even got him to play along with it once and get into character for a little segment on my phone. But I wasn't making fun of him that day at Anfield. His four goals were absolutely stunning. They made everybody sit up and take notice of him.

He's been a great addition to our side. He's a real Arsenal player with a lovely touch and great aware-ness. He plays balls that no one else will see; it took me a while to learn to read him. I noticed that Craig Bellamy said he had studied him when he played at

Zenit St Petersburg and that he was delighted when he moved to the Premier League. When Bellamy was asked to play on the left side of midfield for Manchester City, he said it was studying Arshavin's movement in that position that had enabled him to do it.

That was one of the best games I have ever been involved in, even though it felt like a defeat because Benayoun made it 4–4 with the last kick of the game. But it was a brilliant match. A high-quality match full of breathtaking football. Those are the kinds of games you want to be involved in. The kind you will always remember. It's not as good as winning trophies but it's part of why we love to be footballers.

At the end of the season, the Boss said that if we did not win a trophy in the next one or two years, his strategy for the club would have failed. The last time we'd won a major honour was 2005, and the Boss said he was putting his faith in the young players at the club to set that right. 'Now is the most important moment in the life of this club,' he said, 'and we have to be strong and support this team.'

I got my share of that support with my new contract. There was a lot of pressure for me when I arrived at the club at the age of sixteen when nobody had heard of me, but the contract made me feel as though my hard work had paid off. I knew in the summer of 2009 that I still had plenty to do and that it wasn't as if I'd achieved anything yet, but I was getting closer.

Most of all, I'd like to repay everyone at Arsenal for the faith they have in me and the way they have looked after me over the years. At the end of 2008–09 I was confident we could win things. Every time we came out of the changing room at the training ground my eye went straight to a new picture they'd put up of all of us running towards Almunia after the shoot-out in Rome. It's one of my favourite pictures. It shows the emotion and how much hard work we put in to get there.

Sometimes, when I was doing warm-downs after training at the end of that season, trying not to think about what might have been if some of us had stayed injury-free, I looked around at the others and found myself thinking, 'We have got some bloody good players here.' I was sure we could win things if we just started to believe it.

Seventeen

When I got back from the World Cup in Germany in 2006, I didn't really think about what my international future held or even whether I had one. I was happy to be back home, to be concentrating on Arsenal and trying to push for appearances in the first team. I put England to the back of my mind.

Sven-Göran Eriksson had left as England manager after our World Cup exit and his assistant Steve McClaren had taken over. Steve had done well as Sven's assistant and the FA decided they wanted to go for continuity. I didn't really consider whether this had any particular implications for me. I knew that I just needed to think about Arsenal.

A month or so after we had got home from the World Cup, I was having a meal with Mel and a couple of my old Southampton teammates when my mobile rang. It was Steve McClaren. He was very friendly but he said he wasn't going to pick me in the senior squad for the friendly against Greece which would be his first game in charge. The Under-21s had a game against Moldova and he said he wanted me to play in that.

That was fine with me. I wasn't expecting to play for the seniors. It wasn't as if I felt I'd been snubbed. I imagine McClaren had had far more difficult calls to make that week, mainly the one to David Beckham. He told Beckham, who had already resigned the England captaincy, that he wasn't going to be in the squad for the Greece game either. Everyone said that was the end of Beckham's England career.

So I was included in the England Under-21 party for the forthcoming game against Moldova at Portman Road. I was delighted about that. It was a relief to get away from the pressure of being in the senior squad for a while. I didn't need any more of that at that stage of my career. The Under-21 lads were much closer to me in age – I was still only seventeen, don't forget – and the media scrutiny was a lot less. I felt much more at home.

I was pleased that McClaren phoned me. It set my mind straight. It didn't leave me confused about where I was going to go and it meant that I hadn't fallen off the radar completely after not playing in the World Cup. McClaren must have seen something he liked in training in Germany. It was good of him to call. I was eating a meal with my mates, David Beckham was getting on a plane to the States with the rest of the Real Madrid *galácticos*. McClaren managed to reach both of us. That's all you want – a bit of communication.

I hadn't played for the Under-21s before anyway, so it felt like a step up for me rather than a demotion, and my debut couldn't really have got off to a better start. I scored after two minutes, a decent header from a Leighton Baines cross that the Moldova goal-keeper could only push into the roof of the net. I celebrated like I'd just scored in the World Cup finals. It was a great feeling.

While the senior team was struggling in the European Championship qualifiers, going through the nightmare of that defeat in Croatia where Gary Neville's backpass bobbled over Paul Robinson's foot for an own goal, I got a decent run in the Under-21s. Peter Taylor was the manager and there was a good atmosphere in the squad. It was great to be involved and to be playing.

The highlight, funnily enough, came when we played against Germany at the BayArena in Leverkusen in October. We were 1–0 up from the first leg and we needed to keep a clean sheet to be sure of qualifying for the Under-21 European Championship in Holland the following summer. I was on the bench but I finally got to run out in an England shirt in Germany in the seventy-seventh minute when the game was still goalless. Three minutes after I came on, Baines pumped a long ball over the Germany defence and I ran on to it, brought it down with my first touch and slotted it past the goalkeeper.

In the last minute, I scored again. This time I got the ball in our own half, knocked it past their right-back and set off for goal. No one caught me, and when I was about ten yards out I opened my body and curled it round the keeper.

Sky interviewed me and Nigel Reo-Coker after the game and all they could talk about was how my goals had reminded them of Thierry Henry. I didn't mind those comparisons at all. Training with him was obviously paying off.

That win over Germany was Peter Taylor's last game in charge. He was replaced by Stuart Pearce, and a few weeks after he took over Stuart rang me to say he had spoken to Arsène Wenger and that he was aware of the problems I was having with my shoulder popping out of joint all the time. He understood the need for me to get it sorted out and had accepted that I would need an operation on it in the spring of 2007.

That ruled me out of the European Under-21 Championship in Holland, where we went out in the semi-finals to the hosts. We were within a minute of making the final when the Dutch scored an equalizer. Then we lost a marathon penalty shoot-out 13–12. I was so disappointed for the lads and for myself, too. Even though I wasn't in Holland, I still felt part of what that Under-21 team achieved.

I didn't think about the senior team much for the whole of that season. McClaren was picking players like David Bentley, Shaun Wright-Phillips and Aaron Lennon on the right of midfield. And in May 2007 he swallowed his pride and recalled Beckham to the squad for the games against Brazil and Estonia. I was a long way out of the frame.

But the senior team continued to struggle. England lost in Russia and then again in November at home to Croatia and failed to qualify for the 2008 European Championship. I watched the Croatia game on the television. I wasn't bitter at not being involved. I didn't expect to be there.

McClaren lost his job after that Croatia defeat and Fabio Capello was appointed the new manager. I wasn't picked in the squad for his first two games, friendlies in February and March 2008 against Switzerland and France, but I was still developing and I knew that if I was getting picked most weeks for Arsenal, I'd have a chance with England.

At the end of the 2007–08 season, while the rest of the best players in Europe went off to Austria and Switzerland for the European Championship, England had lined up friendlies against the USA at Wembley, and Trinidad and Tobago in Port of Spain. Some time in the middle of May, Warwick called me to say he thought I might have a chance of getting in the squad, and when it was announced a week or so later, I was in.

Mr Capello didn't phone me to let me know or anything like that. He doesn't go in for frills. I was excited to be involved, partly because it held out the prospect of getting another cap for my country and ticking another box in my recovery from not having kicked a ball at the World Cup, and partly because it was a new manager. A new manager with a great reputation.

I felt much more at home in the senior squad than I had done in Germany. I had a bit of experience of what everything was like. I knew some of the other players now and I knew what was coming in terms of the media and the training and the routine so I wasn't too nervous. There was also a feeling that Mr Capello was ready to trust the younger players and players who were in form. There was a real sense of opportunity around the place.

There were big differences to the way it had been under Mr Eriksson. It became obvious straight away that Mr Capello was very strict. It was like being in the presence of a headmaster. If you are eating and you look over to where he is and he is looking at you, you look down and eat straight away. You're shit scared of him basically.

Every player reacts in a different way, but I think that's what you need from a manager. Maybe McClaren was a bit too matey with the players. I only had experience of him when he was Sven's assistant, but he called people by their Christian names or their nicknames. Jamie Carragher was always Carra, Steven Gerrard was Stevie G, Beckham was Becks, and so on. Mr Capello doesn't go in for that kind of familiarity. From the outset he called Gerrard . . . well, Gerrard. He called Beckham Beckham. I think players like that kind of firm management. If you don't respect him, you won't play for him. And you knew straight away with Mr Capello that if you weren't playing well you weren't going to be in his squad or his plans. He is ruthless like that.

There is this presence about him. It makes you believe that if you follow what he says, you will win things. And when he believes in you, you play better and your confidence goes up. But woe betide you if you put a foot out of line off the pitch. Don't touch your mobile phones in his presence, especially around dinner. That is a very serious no-no. Emile Heskey fell foul of that one during the World Cup qualifiers when Mr Capello caught him texting someone during dinner. I wasn't there because I was injured but I read about it in the papers like everyone else. Mr Capello got up and yelled and chucked something when he saw what Emile was doing. I would not have liked to be in his shoes at that moment.

I had one close shave straight away with the discipline side of things. When I met up with the squad before the USA game we were allowed to play nine holes of golf at The Grove, which is our training base for home games. I got Dad to bring my clubs, and because there's a very strict food regime under Mr Capello I was really craving some crisps, just something different from the rather bland food we're allowed to eat officially, so I told Dad to bring a snack along with him too.

Dad brought some Pringles for me, but as he was lifting the clubs out of the boot I noticed with horror that Mr Capello was watching everyone like a hawk. Dad was about to grab the Pringles and hand them to me. He realized just in time that that would be a serious error. He had them in his hand but he put them back in the boot of the car as nonchalantly as he could. It was all very cloak-and-dagger.

The food we're officially allowed is OK, it just gets a bit boring. There's a lot of pasta and chicken. Sometimes the lads get a bit stir crazy with it. During the build-up to one match, some of us snuck in some Nando's on the quiet. That was a seriously nerve-racking episode. Everybody kept expecting Mr Capello to burst out of the shadows as the players were eating their food. I was so nervous that when the food arrived I could hardly eat it.

I didn't play in the home game against the USA but I did get on against Trinidad and Tobago. I got a great reception at the Hasely Crawford Stadium because there were suggestions that I was related to the great West Indian batsman Sir Clyde Walcott. My dad thinks there is a connection. Sir Clyde, who died in 2006, wasn't so sure. Whatever the truth of it, the crowd liked the name.

I've never really checked out my Caribbean heritage. My dad's family is from Jamaica but my grandfather had already left by the time Dad was born and I've never been there. I'm not really curious about it. It feels very distant. I'm close to my Jamaican grandfather but he lives in Carterton in Oxfordshire (I switched the Christmas lights on in the town in 2006). It's not as if I need to fly out to the Caribbean to visit him and my grandma.

I did OK in Port of Spain. I got on for the last

twenty minutes and managed a couple of shots. One of them was more like a pass back to the goalkeeper, actually. But we were 3–0 up after fifty minutes and it was hard to inject urgency into the action by the time I got on. The significance of the game was more symbolic for me. It reminded everyone I was still around, still worthy of consideration for an England place after the false start of the World Cup. For a lot of the lads it was the last game of a long, hard season. Everyone knew that the important games were coming at the other end of the summer.

Eighteen

I wasn't involved in the first England squad of the new season for a friendly against the Czech Republic, but I was called up for the games that mattered, the first two matches in our campaign to qualify for the 2010 World Cup in South Africa. The first was away against Andorra, but that was really just a warm-up for the second one, the game against Croatia in Zagreb that followed four days later. I didn't think I'd start in either, but there was a chance I might get a game against Andorra because it was a match we were expected to win comfortably.

I say that, but we had played them in qualifying for the European Championship when McClaren was manager and it was, apparently, a thoroughly unpleasant experience that was more like a bear-baiting event than a football match.

When Andorra played countries like England that brought a lot of travelling fans, they staged their home games at the Olympic Stadium in Barcelona. The game there under McClaren was mainly memorable for the treatment the England fans dished out to the England players and the manager. I wasn't involved at that stage, but the England fans had been growing increasingly dissatisfied with McClaren's management and the team's performances, and all their resentments were vented during that match. The squad members who hadn't made the bench and were sitting in the stands were given so much stick they had to move. The abuse rained down from the terraces. A lot of the lads who were there said they had never seen anything like it before.

We won that game in the end, but because it had been a struggle it was still treated as a defeat by some. McClaren was rattled afterwards and walked out of his post-match press conference after about thirty seconds. Then, when he spotted one of the England press lads walking out of the stadium, he joked with the bus driver that he should try to run him over and the papers made a big thing out of that too. The episode was one of the low points of his spell as England boss.

The main thing was to avoid any repeat of that. It was important that Mr Capello got off to a good start in his first competitive match so that we went to Croatia in good heart. Any hiccup against these minnows and the heat would be on the new boss straight away. Because of that, most people were expecting Mr Capello to stick with David Beckham on the right side of midfield, to use his experience and his quality as a steadying influence to make sure we got through the game without any alarms.

I did OK in training. In fact, there was one session before we left when I got the ball, accelerated past a couple of players and scored. Maybe that stuck in the manager's mind a little bit. I am sure Beckham was in the starting line-up until that point, but after that Mr Capello started alternating the two of us in what I assumed was the starting line-up. I still didn't think I'd start. Neither did my dad. He didn't even come to the game because he didn't have a clue I was going to play.

We only find out the team on the day of the game, and when we had our squad meeting Mr Capello told me I was starting. I was delighted. I knew it was a big chance for me, although at the time I didn't realize quite how big. I was just buzzing to be playing. But somewhere in the back of my mind I was thinking that they were playing me so they could rest David for the big one against Croatia the following Wednesday.

Beckham was great with me when the team was announced. There was not a hint of him sulking because he had been left out. There was no sense that he was upset at missing out. In fact, it was the opposite. He had been very kind to me in the run-up to the World Cup when I was new to everything, and I got to know him a bit better when he trained with Arsenal for a spell after his first season at the LA Galaxy. He came and talked to me when the team was announced for the Andorra game and told me that as long as I played my own game, I would be fine. He told me to do everything I could to enjoy it and then I would play my best football. He didn't bring any feeling at all that the two of us were rivals.

I was pleased with the way the game went. I wasn't too nervous and I played well. Andorra stuck ten men behind the ball and made it difficult for us but we kept plugging away and the fans stayed patient. They were getting a little restless when we went in at half-time with the scoreline still at 0–0, but once Joe Cole, who came on at the interval, put us ahead it became a fairly straightforward victory. It might only have been Andorra but I had finally played in my first competitive match for England, and we had won.

We stayed in Barcelona for a couple of days before we went to Croatia. That was a good plan. We didn't want to be exposed to the intensity of feeling in Zagreb any earlier than necessary. Better to stay in a neutral environment for as long as possible. I'd played well against Andorra but I still didn't think I'd start in Zagreb. I thought Mr Capello would want to field his biggest players, especially after what had happened against Croatia in the last qualifying campaign and all the Wally with the Brolly stuff that came McClaren's way.

In fact both our matches against Croatia in the Euro 2008 qualifiers had turned into humiliating defeats, for different reasons. In the away game, the first meeting, the intensity of the atmosphere in the stadium in Zagreb seemed to catch England by surprise. Croatia had never lost a home game in a competitive match and they and their fans were incredibly fired up for the match. We got a bad break with Gary Neville's own goal and then they scored a second to seal the result.

McClaren never really recovered from that result, but England still went into the final qualifier at Wembley needing only a draw to qualify. But we didn't draw with the Croats. With the help of Beckham, who came on as a substitute, we recovered from 2–0 down to draw level at 2–2, but then we conceded again, and that time there was no way back. We slipped to a 3–2 defeat, and McClaren ensured he was vilified more than he would otherwise have been when he sheltered under an umbrella on the touchline.

There was no chance of that accusation ever being levelled at Mr Capello. With him, it was clear to me immediately it was all about substance. He didn't care about a player's reputation or how big a name he had or how many caps he had won. He picked players on form, and that was it. No sentiment. No friendships. Cold and clinical. There was about as much chance of him getting pally with the players as there is of Gary Neville going on a night out with Carlos Tévez.

I knew I'd played well against Andorra and I hoped that I hadn't let anyone down, but for twenty-four hours after the match I still thought Beckham would probably start in Croatia. It was England's biggest game since . . . well, since the last time we played Croatia, but this time it was crucial to our hopes of reaching the World Cup finals. Somehow the stakes always seem to be that little bit higher when it's the World Cup you're trying to get to rather than the European Championship.

Once again, we didn't find out the team until the day of the game in Zagreb, but I had begun to hope I might have an outside chance of playing. We trained in Barcelona the day before we flew to Croatia and Mr Capello was swapping me, Beckham and Bentley around on the right side of the midfield in the team that looked like it would start. I was getting swapped less than the other two so that gave me a bit of encouragement.

The day before the game and on the day of the game itself, I always prepare as if I am starting. I get myself into the right state of mind and ready myself physically and mentally as if my name is going to be on the list Mr Capello puts up at the team meeting. If you're not on it, it's a big anti-climax, but it's better to have to deal with that than being caught by surprise if you're selected. The day of the Croatia game, I sat in the team meeting with my fingers crossed, and when he put the team sheet up, I was on it.

It was a big call for him to play me ahead of Beckham. A lot of people were saying it was an occasion that demanded experience above everything else. I could offer many things, but experience wasn't one of them. I knew the atmosphere was going to be intense, and when we got to the Maximir Stadium that Wednesday night the home fans were already making a hell of a noise. It was as feverish an atmosphere as I've ever experienced, right up there with the racket the Fenerbahçe fans made.

I have never felt so nervous before a game as I did that night. Beckham was great with me again. He had a chat with me in the dressing room and tried to get the same message across: that I had to play my own game and enjoy myself. The coaching staff were giving me a lot of encouragement too. I'm sure they all realized that, even though I had experienced all the hoopla of the World Cup, I had never actually played in a game like this before. This was a big step up for me.

I was all over the place in the first ten minutes. I got caught in possession on the edge of our own box, the ball was bouncing off me every time somebody passed it to me, and everything seemed incredibly rushed. The Croatia fans were going nuts. I was thinking, 'Oh bloody hell . . .' I wouldn't say I was panicking, but that was probably only because I didn't have time to panic. Maybe all the hype and the pressure of having played well against Andorra and being expected to do it again got to me a little bit. It was the first time I'd had that kind of expectation.

And then, twenty minutes before half-time, I scored. Mr Capello always likes me to stay out wide, hug the touchline and push right up on the opposing full-back, so when there was a mix-up in the Croatia defence and one defender whacked an attempted clearance into another, the ball squirted clear and came straight to me. I took one touch, then another to get it out from under my feet, and whacked it across the goalkeeper into the corner of the net.

Everything went quiet. The fans were stunned. I stood still for a second. Some people thought the goal must have been disallowed because I didn't react. The truth was, I didn't know what to do. It was a similar feeling to when I scored my first goal in senior football for Southampton against Leeds at Elland Road. I didn't know where to run, what to do with my arms. So I walked round in a circle looking daft until the other England players piled on top of me. That was a great feeling.

From that point on the nerves went and I was a free spirit again. I felt as if I'd been released from the weight of expectation and that anything was possible.

Suddenly, it was half-time. There was jubilation when we came off but I also noticed the England staff looking at me with concern. I realized then that I was limping, and my heart sank. I thought I must have got an injury and that maybe I was only just starting to feel it because the adrenalin had worn off for a minute. But I felt fine. I didn't have any pain. The physios sat me down and took a look at my legs. They flexed my knees. Still no problems. Then they checked my boots and found something bizarre. A stud was missing in my right boot. Actually, the stud had snapped off in the mould of the boot and no one could get it out. And I didn't have any spare boots.

That shows you I was still a bit raw. No spare boots! Most professionals take a couple of spare pairs with them to matches. No one knew what to do. I was going to wear a pair of Rooney's because he wore the same size nines as me, but his foot was a different shape to mine and his boots were broader. So they just told me to wear the same broken boot in the second half. It hadn't done me much harm in the first forty-five minutes after all. So I played the entire second half with a stud missing. I forgot about it almost as soon as the second half started.

Then things started to get surreal. A quarter of an hour after the interval we broke forward again and Heskey got the ball on the edge of the box. He laid it back to Rooney and he rolled a beautifully simple pass out wide to me. I drilled the ball across the keeper to put us two up. The finish was almost the same as the first one. It was like a wonderful recurring dream. I know 'surreal' is an overused word, but it really felt as if this wasn't real. I still didn't really know how to celebrate. Wes Brown was the first England player I saw when I wheeled round so I ran over and jumped on him. It was a brilliant feeling. We were winning in Croatia, we were making a great start to our World Cup qualifying campaign, and I'd scored two goals for my country.

I had a quick look up at the stands in the forlorn

hope I might spot Dad, who had made hasty arrange-
ments to come out to Zagreb after I'd played in
Andorra, but I didn't have a clue where he was so
there was no chance of spotting him. I found out later
that he was in among the Croatia fans, the only black
guy in a sea of angry and dismayed Croats. He told
me that he did stand up and punch the air when I
scored. But he also said he sat back down fairly
quickly. My mum was watching the television on her
own at home in Hertfordshire. Mel's parents didn't
have satellite television so Mel had gone out to a local
pub to watch it.

Rooney put us three up four minutes later and the
game was effectively over. They pulled one back
twelve minutes from the end, but before they had
time to think about mounting any real comeback,
Wayne played a clever pass behind the Croatia
defence that allowed me to spring the offside trap and
run on to it on the right. I took the ball right to left
across the face of the Croatia area, and as their
keeper came out to meet me I slid it past him with my
left foot for my hat-trick.

I tried a slide for my goal celebration this time, but
I messed it up. I didn't care. My first thought was to
thank Rooney for the pass, and I turned round and
pointed to him as he came over to celebrate with me.
He was the provider of all three of my goals and he is

a joy to play with. That night, like most nights, he played beautiful football, and in that moment that was the proudest of my career I wanted to acknowledge his part in what I'd done.

Mr Capello substituted me a couple of minutes after I scored my third goal and brought Beckham on in my place.

After the game, people were saying that my coming of age meant the end for Beckham, but actually it was just the signal for a new beginning. He was not a regular starter after that, it's true, but his importance to the side barely diminished and Mr Capello continued to make it clear how much he valued him. It was a desperately cruel blow when David ruptured his Achilles tendon in March 2010 playing for AC Milan against Chievo and was ruled out of the World Cup.

Even though I had a few minutes to sit on the bench and try to take in what had happened in the final stages of the game, I still struggled to believe it all. When we got back to the dressing room it was bedlam, but I stayed very quiet. I didn't know what to think or say to anyone. It was a mad night. I turned my phone on and I had a ridiculous number of messages. The rest of the lads signed the match ball and presented it to me. It's a precious memento.

I was in demand from the press guys in the mixed

zone afterwards, and in the end I had to break off because I wanted to call my family. My dad had a great night. He went out with Warwick and Colin and some of the journalists to celebrate and they ended up in the bar at the Sheraton Hotel in Zagreb until the early hours. I'm so glad he was there to see it. After all the thousands of miles he had driven during my younger days, it was a little bit of payback. When I spoke to Mum, I had to tell her I'd forgotten my house key and that she was going to have to wait up to let me in. When I got back to Hertfordshire, at about three a.m., she had fallen asleep and there were just the dogs there to meet me.

I loved the plane journey back to England that night. We were all buzzing, and we wound down playing computer games. Maybe that sounds funny to some people. Maybe in the past we would have been drinking all the way back and staggering off the plane bleary-eyed and the worse for wear. Times have changed, I suppose. We played a Socom game the whole way back. It was the SAS against terrorists, and we played five-a-side. Me, JT, Bridgey, Lamps, Rio, Wes, Wayne, Ashley and a couple of others. There was a real feeling of bonding on that journey.

The other players were buzzing about the victory. Most of them had been in the firing line during the low times under McClaren and the manner of the victory in Croatia gave all of us – players and fans – our pride back. And at last I felt I was part of the team. At the World Cup in 2006 I had been a spare part; I felt I turned into a man that night in Zagreb. I watched the tape over and over again when I got home, and as I saw the images on the screen, images of me being submerged by celebrating teammates, I felt like I belonged at last.

Nineteen

I was woken by the phone ringing in my hotel room at The Grove. The voice on the other end sounded nervous. It was one of the England staff. He said I'd missed a team meeting and that I'd better come and sort it out with Fabio Capello. I'd thought the meeting was at 7.30 p.m. but it turned out it had been half an hour earlier. I'd had an afternoon nap and set my alarm too late. I'd slept through the meeting. I could feel my heart thumping in my chest. I had never missed a team meeting before. I was in trouble.

It was the Monday evening before England's friendly against Holland in Amsterdam in August 2009. It was the start of the season building up to the World Cup in South Africa. I was already struggling with a slight back injury I'd picked up in Arsenal's final pre-season match against Valencia a few days earlier. This wasn't quite the start to a crucial year I had been hoping for.

I got downstairs as fast as I could and spoke to one of the coaches. I didn't know what to do. He said I should go and apologize to Mr Capello. I looked around the hotel's public areas but he'd gone. The coach said he had gone back to his room. He told me where the room was so I went up there.

I stood in front of his hotel room door for a few seconds, my heart thumping hard. I knocked on the door. There was a brief wait that seemed like a lifetime. Then Mr Capello opened the door. He stood there, looking at me.

I apologized to him profusely. 'Boss,' I said, 'I'm so sorry I missed the meeting. I misread the time.'

Mr Capello's expression stayed the same. He shrugged his shoulders, then let the door swing shut in my face. He hadn't said a word.

'Oh, fuck me,' I thought. It was much worse than getting a severe bollocking. It was seriously scary.

I went back downstairs and did the rounds. I apologized to Franco Baldini, Mr Capello's number two. He told me not to worry about it. I went to speak to John Terry, the England captain, and he did his best to reassure me. He said a couple of players had missed meetings before and not bothered to apologize so at least I had had the guts to do that. I've no idea if he was telling me the truth or just trying to make me feel better.

My week didn't improve. I was supposed to be released the next day to go back to Arsenal because of my injury. This had been agreed between Arsenal and the England medical staff, but it soon became apparent the message had not got through to Mr Capello. I went to say goodbye to him on the Tuesday morning and wish him all the best for the match and he looked puzzled. Puzzled in an angry kind of way.

'What?' he said.

'I've got an injury, boss,' I said. 'The staff have told me to go home.'

'No,' Mr Capello said. 'You are coming to Holland.'

So I went. I didn't train when we got to Amsterdam the night before the match because the injury prevented that. I did a bit of the pre-match warm-up out on the pitch but my back was too sore to do any more than that. Then I sat on the bench for the duration of the 2–2 draw. I never even got out of my seat to warm up. It seemed a slightly curious way of going about things because I could have gone back to Arsenal the day before and concentrated on starting my recovery.

Back at Arsenal, the Boss wasn't exactly impressed. He was still annoyed that I had had to spend a large part of my summer in Sweden with England Under-21s playing in the European Championship. I had already played for the senior team earlier in the summer in the World Cup qualifying victories away to Kazakhstan and at home to Andorra but Stuart Pearce wanted me to go Sweden and no one said no.

I didn't blame the Boss for being wary of my England commitments. At the start of the 2008–09 season I had been playing my best football both for Arsenal and for England. I scored the hat-trick against Croatia and played in the qualifiers at home to Kazakhstan and away to Belarus. It was brilliant. I had heard all the stuff in previous years about how a lot of the players didn't enjoy their time with England, either because of the managerial regime or the stick they got from the press, or even the way they were booed sometimes at the old Wembley, but I was revelling in everything that came with playing for my country.

Then I went away with England again in November 2008 and dislocated my shoulder in the final training session before our friendly match against Germany in Berlin. I had been looking forward to that game so much. It was a chance to play in the Olympic Stadium where the World Cup Final had been in 2006. It was a chance to play against Germany, our biggest rivals. I was really excited about it.

It was raining the night before the game when we trained at the stadium. With only ten minutes of the session left, I was in the corner with the ball and Scott Parker came up behind me and nudged me. I lost my footing and fell on my right shoulder. It popped out and popped back in. I stayed quiet. If someone had looked at my face, they could have told I was hurting. And I was thinking, 'What the bloody hell's going on now?' I had never done my right shoulder before. It had always been the left.

Somebody asked if I was OK and I said I'd play on. I was so desperate to play against Germany. I just hoped it would be all right but I knew it could go again at any minute. Sure enough, we were finishing off the game when I got the ball, spun round and put my arm up in the air. There was no one near me but my shoulder just went. I collapsed to the floor and crawled to the corner of the pitch. I was in agony.

The lads stopped for a minute, then played on. Because the stadium was so quiet, the sound of my screams echoed round it. Not very nice for the rest of them, I imagine. But I was in too much pain to worry about that. They pumped me full of painkillers until I was totally out of it, put me in an ambulance and sped me off to the hospital.

It was a fracture/dislocation, and I don't think I've ever been in so much pain. They corrected the dislocation at the hospital and put me in the most uncomfortable sling ever. The only thing that cheered me up was that Gary Lewin, the England physio, said I could eat whatever I wanted. I had a burger and chips and some rice pudding. I watched *The Terminator* on my laptop and went to bed. I got some sleep, too. I could sleep through a tornado.

I didn't feel too depressed. I was really down when I had the operation on my other shoulder, but I had come back from that fine so I knew I would be stronger once the operation was done on my right one and I had convalesced. I knew I had to try to enjoy the process of getting back to fitness. I have seen players get really down during rehab and it takes them even longer than it should to regain fitness. I knew I had to stay positive. I used my Arsenal teammate Tomas Rosicky, who was returning from a long-term injury, as my role model. He came in every day, smiling and happy to see the other players. Staying positive certainly helped: my recovery flew by.

The injury in Berlin in November 2008 took eight months out of my England senior career, so, after playing against Kazakhstan and Andorra in June 2009, part of me wanted to go to Sweden with the Under-21s while part of me knew it meant there was a risk I'd be storing up trouble for the following season. Arsène Wenger mapped out the potential problems with what I was being asked to do when he spoke to the press. He said the danger was that I would come back late from the Under-21s, have a shortened pre-season and pick up an injury.

But what could I do? It wasn't up to me to make the decision. Look what happened to David Bentley when he pulled out of an Under-21 tournament: he was vilified for it and condemned as a big-time Charlie. The same thing happened to Gabriel Agbonlahor when he disappeared after the end of a season and didn't return the manager's phone calls. As for me, I just wanted to play for my country.

I kept hearing all this stuff about how I was defying Arsène Wenger by insisting on going to play in Sweden. It was presented as though I was putting my foot down and arguing against the Boss. It just wasn't true. If the Boss had told me to stay at home, I would have stayed at home. But Arsenal would have got into trouble if they'd done that, and, whatever the headlines may have said, that conversation never took place. Mr Wenger didn't say anything to me about not going. He didn't put me under any pressure to pull out or anything like that. There has been speculation since that he was against my going. He may well have expressed that view to Mr Capello and Stuart Pearce, but if those discussions happened, I was never aware of them. The only thing Mr Wenger ever said to me about it was to tell me when I was due back at Arsenal for pre-season training. He also wished me all the best, actually, and said he hoped we won the tournament. People assume he must have been putting obstacles in my way, but he wasn't. Still, the dilemma over whether to select me for the tournament was presented as a classic club v. country battle.

I felt I was being pulled both ways. I didn't know what was going to happen. I was happy doing whatever was decided. I didn't mind. I was happy to let England and Arsenal battle it out. That was all I could do. I couldn't take the lead and dominate the conversation. I didn't want to turn my back on my country and I certainly didn't want to pull out under false pretences. I also felt a loyalty to Steve Wigley, Pearce's assistant, who had been one of my coaches at Southampton. I felt I owed him a debt. I didn't want to let him down.

I couldn't question the decision made by Mr Capello and Stuart Pearce. I believe Mr Capello's theory is that when an England team is involved in a tournament, they should do everything they can to try to win it. That's the attitude they adopt in Italy. Their view is that if the Under-21 side wins a tourna-ment, that experience of winning will filter through to the senior side and gradually foster a winning mentality. So they put their best young players forward for the Under-21s in a tournament situation irrespective of whether they also play for the senior team.

Mr Capello and Pearce seemed happy for me to spend my entire summer playing football, and I didn't object. I loved playing for the Under-21s and there was a great spirit in the camp. But after all the fuss that was made about me going, when I got to Sweden things did not go quite as I had anticipated.

Five days after I had played against Andorra for the senior team, I was lining up for the Under-21s in our first game of the European Championship, against Finland in Halmstad. I was playing on the right, James Milner was on the left and Agbonlahor was on his own up front. We struggled a little bit in the first half and I didn't have the best forty-five minutes, but all of us were in the same boat. No one played well. We weren't at it, I don't know why. We came in at the interval and Pearce told me he was taking me off and replacing me with Fraizer Campbell.

I knew I hadn't played well. I even told the press later in the tournament that I'd been so bad even my parents had booed me off. But I wasn't happy about Pearce's decision. No player is happy when he gets dragged off at half-time. I thought there was still plenty of time for me to make an impact. It was 1–1 and there was everything to play for. I felt worse about it because of the fact that my participation in the tournament had become such a focal point for everyone. They had won this battle to get me out there and made a big deal out of it, and now the manager had picked on me after the team had had a bad half.

We won the game 2–1 – Micah Richards got the winner with a header – and I hoped I'd start the next game, the big one against Spain, so I could put the disappointment behind me. The team was announced on the morning of the game. The line-up came up on the projector at the team meeting in the hotel. My name wasn't there. You should have seen my face. I'm not really a sulker or a dummy-spitter, but in that instant – and I know you absolutely cannot do this – I felt like walking out of the room.

I was so disappointed. That's the worst I've ever felt when a team has been selected. Everyone can have a bad game and I was dismayed about how I was being treated. I didn't think I was being shown enough support. I had supported them by not being awkward about going, not making a fuss and being professional. I know that doesn't give me any guarantees, but I felt that it was slightly curious to be making an example of me now.

I don't know what was behind it, really. All sorts of wild thoughts went through my mind. Maybe it was Stuart Pearce trying to make a statement about how he was a strong manager by leaving out one of the team's high-profile players. Perhaps he thought it would play well with people at the FA who would see he wasn't star-struck. It might strengthen his case to succeed Mr Capello whenever that time came.

That's fine. Everybody has their own agendas. But I needed support from them because I felt there was pressure on me going into that tournament. There had been all the debate about whether I should go or not, and the organizers had used me as one of the faces of the tournament. I understood suddenly what it was like for someone like Beckham who has the spotlight on him all the time and has to cope with the weight of expectation.

I suppose that's just part of what happens as your career develops. Things that used to be simple aren't so simple any more. They get complicated by other issues. When Beckham was at the 1998 World Cup, the England manager at the time, Glenn Hoddle, told the press he felt Beckham wasn't properly focused, which led to all sorts of speculation about his private life. It seems to me that the manager was playing games with him when really it should have been just about football.

On a much smaller scale, what happened in Sweden gave me a brief glimpse into this world, into what Beckham has to deal with. Because of my hat-trick against Croatia and the publicity I'd had around the 2006 World Cup, I was probably the highest-profile player in the tournament in Sweden, along with Barcelona's young Spanish star Bojan, and I felt I was being singled out unfairly for criticism.

I didn't walk out of the meeting. I sat there and stewed. I felt like I had been stabbed in the back and I made up my mind that I'd confront Stuart Pearce about it. I didn't do it that afternoon because it was a very important match and I didn't want to make it appear as if I thought my situation was bigger than the game itself. I didn't think that, but I needed to clear the air with him because my head was spinning.

I made my point on the pitch first. Pearce had picked Adam Johnson instead of me for the Spain game, but when the score was still goalless midway through the second half, he brought me on. Five minutes later we went one up with a great goal from Fraizer Campbell, and soon after I sprinted past Raul Garcia and cut a cross back from the byline for James Milner, who smashed it in. We won 2–0, qualified for the semi-finals with a game to spare, and I got the headlines for the right reasons.

Pearce was unrepentant when he was asked about

whether he still felt justified in having left me out. 'I said before we left England that Theo would be treated the same as the other twenty-two in the squad,' Pearce said. 'What I do ask for is a reaction if they do get left out. You saw what Theo was about as a man and a player. He reacted the way I thought he would.'

That was good to hear, and I felt a great sense of relief that things were looking up. But I still spoke to Pearce the next day and told him I wasn't happy. He understood that, and he said I had sent out a great message to the squad by reacting in the way I had and coming off the bench to make an impact. He said to the squad later that I had showed great courage. He talked about seeing my face when my name wasn't on the team list and how dignified I had been about it. It made me extra glad I had kept my mouth shut at the time.

The thing was, everything else was going so well. I was really enjoying the tournament experience. It was more enjoyable than the World Cup in some ways because all of the lads in Sweden were a similar age to me. We were always in the games room after meals, playing table tennis and Mario Kart. There was a lot of darts and a lot of bonding. We had a competition to see who could grow the best moustache. I won it. I got on well with absolutely everybody: Martin Cranie, my old teammate from my Southampton days; Richard Stearman, the Wolves defender (who was runner-up in the moustache contest); Adam Johnson, who's at Manchester City now; Joe Hart and Gibbsy as well. They were a great bunch of lads.

One day we decided to hire bikes and ride en masse to the nearest McDonald's. We'd got sick of having the same kind of food day after day so someone got on Google to find out where the nearest McDonald's was. It was a good few miles but we all made it. I hadn't had a Big Mac for a few years, so the one I had that day in Sweden tasted very good indeed.

I didn't really expect to start the final group game, against Germany. Everybody was already thinking about the semis by then so the manager gave some other people a run-out. I came off the bench with about half an hour to go but it was already 1–1 by then and both teams were relatively happy to settle for a draw. That result meant we finished top of the group and played Sweden in Gothenburg in the semis.

We were confident going into the game. It showed. We went ahead after fifty-three seconds through Cranie. Then Nedum Onuoha put us 2–0 up and Mattias Bjärsmyr sliced the ball into his own net after I'd drilled a cross into the box and Lee Cattermole had flicked it on, to give us a three-goal lead. It wasn't even half-time. The crowd booed the Swedes off at the interval. I didn't think there was any way back for them.

But what is it about 3–0 leads and how vulnerable they can make you? I had seen it happen to AC Milan when Liverpool came back at them in the 2005 Champions League Final in Istanbul, and the same thing happened to us in Gothenburg. I suppose you allow yourself to think you've won it, and somewhere in your subconscious you relax. Once the Swedes got one goal back, we grew a little nervous and they still had nothing to lose so they kept going for it. Then they got another goal back, and then another. They scored three goals in thirteen minutes and suddenly we were clinging on for extra time.

We made it, but extra time was uncomfortable too. It was inevitable that the momentum would be with the Swedes after the comeback they had staged. Their striker, Marcus Berg, who was one of the players of the tournament, hit the crossbar and Joe Hart made three brilliant saves to keep us in the game and take the tie to a penalty shoot-out.

In the circumstances it was a relief to get to penalties, but England's record in shoot-outs didn't exactly fill anyone with confidence. It wasn't just the senior team that had a depressing record. The

Under-21s had lost that epic shoot-out with Holland in Heerenveen two years earlier. Stuart Pearce didn't have many fond associations with penalties either. He might have scored against Spain in Euro 96, but he missed one of the kicks in the shoot-out with Germany that cost England a place in the 1990 World Cup Final – probably the most heartbreaking penalties defeat we have ever had.

We all got a terrible sense of déjà vu when Milner took our first penalty, slipped as he planted his foot and sliced his shot high and wide – a bit like Beckham had once done in the shoot-out against Portugal. In that instant it felt as if this penalty hoodoo that has cursed us so often was back again and that there was no escaping it. The idea that we had got ourselves into this mess by letting our three-goal lead slip was still nagging at me too.

Berg stepped up to take their first kick and I thought there was no way he'd miss. He was in unstoppable form, his confidence was high. I thought he was a certainty to score. He smashed his penalty right down the middle, hard and true, but Hart saved it with his legs and hope came flooding back into us. Hart took the next penalty himself and scored with an absolute cracker into the roof of the net before the Swedes levelled it at 1–1.

We scored another two, they scored another two.

Although, just to add another twist, Hart was booked for talking to the Swedish penalty takers before the Swedes' fourth penalty which meant that he would miss the final if we got through. He knew exactly what that meant but he didn't show any emotion. He didn't wobble one bit. He was absolutely brilliant in that shoot-out.

So it was effectively sudden death. And now it was my turn. I didn't feel quite as nervous as I had done when I stepped up for Arsenal against Roma, but it still wasn't easy. I took ages to get the ball on the spot. I kept putting it down and it kept rolling into a tiny divot. In the end I got it where I wanted it and walked back. I thought I'd put it to the same side as I had done in Rome, into the bottom left-hand corner. I ran up, got a good connection on it, and the keeper went the wrong way. What a great feeling that was.

If the Swedes' next penalty taker, Rasmus Bengtsson, missed then we were through. But he didn't miss. Kieran Gibbs took our next kick and rolled it into the corner as cool as you like. That meant the heat was on Guillermo Molins. It wasn't a bad effort but he struck it a fraction wide and it hit the outside of the post and cannoned away to safety. We had finally won a penalty shoot-out.

It was the first time England had been to the final

of the Under-21 tournament for twenty-five years and we all rushed to Joe Hart to congratulate him, and also to commiserate with him. No one had ever heard of a goalkeeper being booked for talking to players. I don't know how the referee justified that. Ungentlemanly conduct, perhaps, but it seemed very harsh. It was the same ref who had booked him for time-wasting in the opening game against Finland. It took a bit of the gloss off the victory, particularly as we knew that Agbonlahor and Campbell would also be suspended for the final against Germany. The mood in the dressing room was still great because of what we had achieved and the way we had recovered after blowing that three-goal lead, but I felt bad for the three players who were going to miss out.

After the game, I went to see my family, Mel and Mel's mum, who were waiting around outside the stadium. I had to go outside the perimeter to get to them and it got a bit crowded with a lot of people jostling and shoving so I took them back past the barrier so we could have a quiet chat. They let Mel through but not Mum and Dad or Mel's mum. That was fair enough. They didn't have passes.

So I was having a snatched conversation with Mel when suddenly this steward grabbed her by the arm and tried to drag her away. He didn't say 'excuse me' or anything, he just started manhandling her. I lost it.

I don't lose it very often, and it was probably just the emotion of what had gone on during the last couple of hours, not to mention the last couple of weeks, but I pushed him, then pushed him again. Hard. I shoved him into a fence, and at that point he backed off. I hardly ever lose my temper, but I did that day.

The tournament had given me an insight into the pressures the leading England players have to deal with all the time. I felt like I was one of the leaders of that Under-21 side, or at least one of the higher-profile players, and it got to me a little bit. I had never been in that situation before and I didn't deal with it that well. I paid a bit too much attention to all the publicity. I thought too much about trying to do well in the tournament, about trying to stand out, for myself and for the team. I was too hung up on trying to make an impact, and when I had that early set-back, it felt more dispiriting than it should have done.

The final against Germany in Malmö was an anti-climax. I enjoyed it in one way because I got to play in my favourite position, up front ahead of a five-man midfield. Arsenal's chief scout, Steve Rowley, was in the crowd to represent the club and keep tabs on how I was doing, and I was pleased with the way I played in attack. I wasn't so pleased with the result.

Only two players survived from the team that had started the match against Germany in the group stage, and we were weakened by the players we were missing. But when you've got a midfield of Fabrice Muamba, Lee Cattermole, Mark Noble, James Milner and Adam Johnson you're entitled to feel you're going to be a match for most young sides in the world.

We were for a while. Cranie headed over early and I fired one just over from a narrow angle. I had another glimpse of a chance after ten minutes when I was one on one with Germany's last defender, but he robbed me with a great challenge. We were playing really well, but midway through the first half Germany scored a terrific goal and it knocked us back.

Two minutes after half-time, the game slipped away from us. Germany won a free-kick more than thirty yards out and the Watford goalkeeper Scott Loach, who was deputizing for Joe Hart, misjudged the flight of the ball. He didn't get his body behind it and could only get a weak hand to it. As he turned to watch the ball, it trickled over the line in slow-mo.

We had a few half-chances after that. Cattermole hit the bar with a thirty-yard thunderbolt and there were a couple of occasions when I thought I had broken through only to be denied at the last second by a German tackle or block. But the breakthrough wouldn't come and the Germans scored two more late on to leave the scoreline looking like a rout when it had never been that. They were a good team, but I didn't think they deserved to win the tournament.

There was a lot of talk afterwards about Pearce's antics on the touchline. He was getting incredibly animated apparently, to the point that some people said it looked undignified, but I didn't really notice it. You can always hear him from the sidelines, that's true, but he's a passionate guy so you expect him to be animated. You know what? After all the little battles we had out in Sweden, I enjoyed playing for him in the end. He's a good coach.

I certainly learned a lot from that European Championship. It was a proper tournament experience for me, right at the heart of things, not standing on the outside with my face pressed against the glass like I had been at the 2006 World Cup. I wasn't homesick. I wasn't lonely. I loved feeling the tournament develop as we made our way through it to the final. It gave me a taste for it. It made me want that place in Mr Capello's squad for South Africa more than ever.

Twenty

There is one statistic that sums up the frustration that welled up in me in the first half of the 2009–10 season more than any other: I didn't play a full ninety minutes for Arsenal until 9 December, and that was in a dead rubber Champions League group game against Olympiakos in Athens when we had already qualified for the second round of the competition.

The first half of the campaign was like an extended medical report for me. I was less a footballer, more a hospital patient. At the end of the season I got a text from the medical guys at the club that was a record of just what I'd missed. It was like an end-of-term school report where they tell you how many days you've been late and missed registration. 'Missed six weeks with side strain from 8 August,' it said. 'Then missed four weeks with medial knee ligament from 17 October. Then missed three weeks with side strain from 27 December. You missed a total of 103 training days.' There it was in stark detail, the diary of the walking wounded.

I was injured even before the season began. I don't think playing for the Under-21s in the summer helped because subconsciously, on both the club's part and mine, there is a desire to take short-cuts when you're getting ready for the new season. I needed a rest after the tournament so I didn't have as long as most of my Arsenal teammates in pre-season.

I didn't play my first pre-season game until a week before we were due to open our Premier League challenge, at Everton on 15 August. The club had arranged a high-profile match against Valencia in the Mestalla on 8 August and I hadn't been on the pitch long when I overstretched as I was trying to reach a pass and damaged muscle fibres in my right side. It was one of those strange injuries that everyone seemed to find hard to diagnose. Arsenal's medical people said it was the kind of strain that usually affects fast bowlers in cricket. It shouldn't happen to a footballer.

The initial prognosis wasn't too bad. It was only supposed to keep me out for a few weeks. Then I came in one morning and it had worsened. I don't know if I had slept in a strange position or what, but it turned out to be a real setback. And so I settled into the routine of the injured. I would come in to the training ground every day as usual. They would immobilize my back and then stretch the hell out of it. When I was improving, I'd go to the gym to do strengthening work on it. Maybe even work on the bike a bit. But usually it was massage, immobilize and the odd bit of ice.

Arsenal's fitness coach, Tony Colbert, hates having players on the bike. He wants to get players out on the pitch straight away. I couldn't do much shoulder work because of the back so they had to get me out on the pitch. I rushed it a bit. I was doing a sprinting activity after having a week's training with Tony, and then I went to turn and felt another sharp pain in my side. That was another setback. Again I tried to keep a smile on my face, remembering how Tomas Rosicky had dealt with his extended injury problems.

It's nice to have other players around you when you're injured. That's a bit selfish, I know, but it's good to have a bit of company. It's better if there are two or three of you because you can feed off each other's progress and set each other extra goals. Later in the season, when Robin Van Persie, William Gallas and Cesc Fabregas all had injuries, there was hardly any space in the medical centre, but when I was out, everyone else seemed to be fit.

Still, Arsène Wenger's not like Bill Shankly used to be with injured players when he was manager of Liverpool in the 1960s and 1970s. Apparently, Shankly wouldn't even look at an injured player. He wouldn't acknowledge his existence. His attitude was that a player was no good to him injured and he wanted the experience to be as miserable as possible so that the player would do everything he could to get back to fitness as soon as possible.

The Boss doesn't behave like that. He comes over to the medics' room to check on everyone fairly often. He wants to get his players back as soon as possible too, and he is always quizzing the physios on how long it's going to be before someone is ready to join the group again. I think they feel a certain amount of pressure when he's hovering over them. But the physios know that if they let a player go back too soon, he runs the risk of breaking down again.

That didn't happen to me. What happened to me was the product of what's best described as an industrial challenge from an opponent. I finally made my first appearance of the season as a substitute in the 6–2 thrashing of Blackburn Rovers at The Emirates on 4 October. I scored five minutes after I came on after Cesc played a great ball through to me. It was a huge boost to my confidence, and even though Mr Capello didn't include me in the squad for the England games against Ukraine and Belarus over the next ten days, I felt my season was about to take off at last when we played our next match at home to Birmingham.

I was in the starting line-up and I began the game well. I forced a good save out of Joe Hart and I felt full of verve and dash. But I was also aware that Birmingham's left-back, Liam Ridgewell, seemed to be targeting me. He had been very aggressive right from the start, and soon enough he took me out. The ball was played into my feet and he came right through me from behind.

If I'd been match sharp, I would have seen him coming and jumped out of the way. But I wasn't in the flow of the action because I had been out for so long, so I was more vulnerable. I didn't see it coming. Technically, I suppose, he got the ball, but he got me too. The result varies when people get you like that. They can injure your ankle, your Achilles tendon or your knee. In my case, it was the knee.

I had a prolonged spell of treatment on the pitch and tried to carry on. I knew something was wrong but I thought I'd try to run it off. I couldn't. The Boss replaced me with Arshavin, and that was me out again. It was an injury to my medial ligament. They said it was the meniscus. It could have been worse. I hadn't snapped the ligament or anything like that, but it felt like a heavy blow. I'd already been out for six weeks. Now I was looking at another month on the sidelines.

I was very down in the dumps for a while. I didn't know what to do. I was on crutches for a couple of days and I couldn't drive. You lose your independence when you get an injury like that. You can't do anything. You have to rely on other people and all the time the season is going on around you and other people are playing well. It's a horrible feeling, but it's one of the things you have to deal with as a footballer.

Arsenal weren't exactly suffering without me. We moved up to second in the Premier League when we beat Spurs at the end of October and there was a lot of optimism around the club. But just when I was coming back after my knee problem, in mid-November, Robin Van Persie got a bad ankle injury during Holland's friendly against Italy and that affected us badly. I came on as a late substitute in the defeat at Sunderland on 21 November, then came off the bench again when we were badly beaten by Chelsea at The Emirates the following weekend.

There is not a lot of point blaming everything on Robin's injury. As it turned out, it kept him out for a lot longer than anyone had expected; in fact he only came back for the last few games of the season. We did miss him, but the other leading title contenders went for long periods of the campaign missing important players too. We can't look at Robin's injury as an excuse. We have to have a squad that can absorb that kind of setback.

I was still searching for full fitness for a while after I came back from the knee ligament injury. I was picking up minor injuries which were probably a result of my body trying to compensate for the other strains and damage I had sustained. I tweaked my hamstring in the defeat to Chelsea and missed the next game against Stoke. And by then it wasn't just me who was becoming incredibly frustrated. The Boss was getting wound up too.

A few days before the Chelsea game I was on the bench for a Champions League tie at home to Standard Liège, and when the Boss was asked in the run-up to the match what he thought my chances were of making Fabio Capello's World Cup squad, he lost his temper. 'For fuck's sake, the World Cup is in June,' he said. 'Is he on holiday until the eleventh of June? You cannot be serious. For me, the big season is with Arsenal, not at the World Cup. We do not pay players to go to the World Cup, we pay the players to do well for Arsenal. The first pride of a man is to do well for the guy who pays you in life, not to go to the World Cup.' That made it pretty clear what the Boss thought about all my injuries. He was fed up with them. He also stressed that it was unusual for a player who had had a poor season with form or injury to have a good World Cup. He highlighted the example of Emmanuel Petit and Patrick Vieira, who both played a full part in winning the Double with Arsenal in 1998 and then won the World Cup with France that summer.

I thought my luck was turning when I played at Olympiakos. I got a nasty kick on my right foot from their midfielder, Leonardo, in the dying minutes and needed treatment on it. I could almost hear groans from the Arsenal bench, but I was fine. I got up and finished the game.

But then, on 27 December, I got injured again playing against Aston Villa. It was another side strain and another three weeks before I even made it back to the bench – another five weeks before I made a start. It was beginning to get to me. As we turned the corner into 2010, dark thoughts started creeping in. Every injury I got, I sank lower and lower. I couldn't see an end to it all.

However much the Boss might have hated it, worries about the World Cup were starting to play on my mind too. I was watching Aaron Lennon and other players like him quite rightly attracting rave reviews for the way they were performing for their clubs and I wasn't even getting the chance to match them. Deep down, you do know it's a World Cup year and you want to play well and try to help the team. When the England team is playing well and people in your position are playing well, you wonder if you are ever going to get back to your level again. All these injuries might upset your whole game completely. The hamstring injury, in particular, worried me, even though it wasn't the worst of my season. Pace is such a big part of my game, hamstring problems are the last thing I need.

It began to feel as though I had had injuries to every part of my leg. I was starting to wonder whether I would ever again be the player I once was. I thought about worst-case scenarios. I thought about what I had done in Croatia and suddenly that seemed a long time ago. I wasn't even twenty-one at that stage and I was wondering if my best days were behind me.

It got to the point where I lied to people about my fitness. I went to Arsenal matches and when people asked me when I was going to be back, I'd say 'maybe next week' when I knew there was very little chance of that happening. I was trying to lift their morale, I think, but probably I was trying to lift mine too. I was just getting sick of being injured and being helpless.

I didn't speak to anyone about the dark thoughts. The odd time I might have opened up to Mel, but not much. When bad things happen, I keep it inside. I try to take my mind off football. When I am fit, I love watching football, but when I'm injured, I hate it. I want to stay away from it. I play golf with my brother if I can, or go to a few theatre shows in the West End, stuff like that. The alternative is sitting at home, thinking bad things.

The truth is I had really started to worry I might not get a chance to play in the World Cup again. I hadn't kicked a ball in 2006 and I'd dreamed of putting that right in South Africa, but now that dream seemed to be slipping away. Even if I did squeeze into the squad, there was no way I'd get back into the first team if I hadn't had the chance to put a good run of form together before the end of the season. It was hard to see light in the darkness.

I was on the comeback trail yet again at the end of February, in and out of the team and feeling a bit sorry for myself, when something happened that put my minor struggles into perspective. I was on the bench at the Britannia Stadium when I saw Stoke's central defender Ryan Shawcross hurl himself into a tackle on Aaron Ramsey, our brilliant young midfield player. Aaron went down and stayed down, and it was clear from the reaction of all around him that something traumatic had happened again.

It was a horrific case of déjà vu. The feeling of sickness in my stomach was the same as when Eduardo sustained his injury at Birmingham City. We soon found out that Aaron's right leg had been broken in the challenge and that it was a very bad break. I was sitting next to Eduardo on the bench and he was in tears when he realized how bad the injury was. It must have brought a lot of bad memories flooding back.

As soon as the tackle happened you could see players near the incident turning away in horror, but Glenn Whelan, the Stoke midfielder, stayed with Aaron and comforted him until the medics came on. He supported him and talked to him to try to get him through the initial pain. Everyone on the Arsenal bench was just numb. No one could believe this was happening to us again.

People talked afterwards about how some clubs target Arsenal because they think that kicking us will jolt us out of our stride. It's the old 'they don't like it up 'em' kind of argument. As far as I'm concerned, it's beyond doubt. People do try and kick us. The injuries we get aren't a coincidence. They're a direct product of the attitude some teams take into matches against us.

It was a bad tackle. Shawcross definitely wanted to

make himself known. I'm not saying he wanted to break his leg because no one would try to do that and everyone could see he was desperately upset when he was walking off the pitch after the referee had given him the red card. But that's the way Stoke are. They try to tackle fairly but they don't mind leaving you hobbling.

It happens quite a lot at places like Stoke, Bolton and Blackburn. If you are a player who influences the game a lot, you will be targeted. Ridgewell was always going to make his presence felt. He was just picking his time to do it. If you are a player at a big club, teams will try to intimidate you by going into these tackles. The home fans love that sort of stuff and that encourages their players to make a name for themselves by throwing themselves into reckless tackles. When I played in the Championship, the fans loved a tackle more than anything. That's the English game.

The result is what happened to Aaron. It's a shame for him because it's changed his career. It's no good just forgetting about the impact that kind of injury has on a player. It's a long, long road back to fitness from something like that.

At least against Stoke we recovered from the shock of what had happened to Aaron. We didn't fold. We went on to win the game 3–1 but it felt like a loss in the dressing room afterwards. No one mentioned the result. Nicklas was trying to text Aaron and some of the others were trying to ring the hospital. It was too soon. No one could reach him. I didn't get a chance to see him in hospital but he came to the training ground a couple of weeks later. He had lost weight. He looked as skinny as a rake. He was in good spirits in the circumstances, but talking to him and realizing what he had ahead of him helped me appreciate that maybe I didn't have it quite so bad after all.

Twenty-one

It was strange, but my season only eventually took a turn for the better on the night I witnessed Arsenal being more comprehensively outplayed than I ever thought possible. It was the last day of March and I was sitting on the bench at The Emirates watching Barcelona rip us to pieces in the first leg of our Champions League quarter-final. I turned to Eduardo, who was sitting next to me, some time in the first half and told him I couldn't believe what I was seeing.

It was easy to see why Barcelona were the reigning champions. They were absolutely magical. All the talk before the game had been about Lionel Messi, but he was actually relatively quiet in that first leg. It was the other nine outfield players who were the problem, Xavi in particular. Most of all, though, it was a brilliant team performance. They played as if they were in total harmony.

At Arsenal, we like to think of ourselves as a team that can play nice football. But in the first half they beat us at our own game. They passed the ball through us and around us. Their movement was magnificent, their running off the ball was unselfish, their fluidity made them hard to track. We barely touched the ball. The more I watched, the more I felt sorry for the lads.

I play the FIFA 10 PS3 game quite a lot, and at times it was like someone in the crowd was controlling each and every one of their players. Some of the stuff they were doing didn't look possible. Xavi makes everything look so easy. He hardly lost the ball. It is the way he lures players in. He does a little touch before they get to him. He sees them coming and gets it and switches it. He creates more space for other players.

You might think I'd have been pleased not to be suffering out on the pitch with my teammates, but actually I was fuming. I hadn't expected to be in the starting eleven because I'd been in and out of the side since returning from injury. But when Arshavin was injured midway through the first half and the Boss brought Eboué on instead of me, I was really angry. I didn't show the annoyance but I did think, 'Where am I now?' Did my injuries mean I had slipped so far down the reckoning that I was now fourth choice on the right? Or even fifth?

Somehow we managed to get to half-time without having conceded a goal. But Zlatan Ibrahimovic scored soon after the break, and then put them 2–0 up after an hour. It looked like it was going to be a rout. Everybody thought it was over, just like it had been when we were so badly beaten by Manchester United in the semi-finals the previous season. With twenty-five minutes left, the Boss brought me on.

I played with controlled anger. I was still upset that Eboué had been brought on before me and I wanted to show the Boss and everyone else in the stadium what I could do. Then, four minutes after I came on, Bendtner slipped a ball past Maxwell and suddenly I was in. I caught Maxwell by surprise a bit, I think, because no one had threatened to get in behind him until then, and suddenly I was through on goal. I hit my shot well but it wasn't really powerful enough and it was too close to the Barcelona keeper Victor Valdes. But it was good enough to beat him. When he went down to try to smother it, it went under his body. I didn't care how it went in. They all count.

The fans went nuts and suddenly the match was transformed. We were all over them and all their fluency and composure deserted them. They weren't stroking the ball around like aristocrats any more, they were clinging on to their lead, and we were tearing into them like fury. Cesc was inspired. He had grown up playing in Barcelona's youth team with a lot of their stars, and even though he had been a doubtful for the game, he played like a man possessed.

Cesc knew that The Emirates leg represented his last chance to influence the tie. He had been booked a minute before half-time for what looked like a good tackle on Sergio Busquets. The yellow card meant he would miss the return leg at the Nou Camp, and he looked distraught. It was made worse by the fact that he shouldn't have been booked. Busquets made an awful lot of the tackle, and after the disgraceful way he subsequently got Inter's Thiago Motta sent off in the semi-final we knew for sure he had a talent for acting. He spent most of that night in north London lying on the floor.

With six minutes left, I got the ball on the right and crossed it. It wasn't a good ball but it bobbled around a bit in their area and Nicklas headed it back across goal for Cesc. Cesc tried to shoot but his leg got tangled up with Carlos Puyol's, and when he went down the referee awarded us a penalty and sent Puyol off. Cesc stepped up to take the kick. He smacked that penalty harder than I've ever seen anybody take one. I'd like to know at what speed it hit the back of the net.

He had already been hobbling a bit, but now Cesc was limping really heavily. It turned out he had broken his leg taking that penalty. I thought he couldn't possibly play on. He could hardly walk. But he refused to go off. There aren't many players who play on with a broken leg. Like I said after the match, Cesc is a soldier.

The return leg at the Nou Camp was less than a week later. No one gave us a chance, so it was a strange build-up. I had been chosen to do the pre-match press conference with the Boss at the stadium, so when our flight touched down in Barcelona I was taken to a car with him and our press chief, Amanda Docherty. Amanda was trying to make conversation and we started talking about the way journalists give players marks out of ten and what criteria they use to judge performance. The Boss said the only way a player would ever get a ten was if he scored four goals. Maybe he was having a premonition.

We got to the stadium and had a look around. There are some steps going down into the tunnel that leads to the pitch, and at the top of the steps there is a chapel. I saw Messi there and stopped to say hello and shake his hand. The Boss just nodded at him, and when we got out on to the pitch he turned to me with a smile and said, 'Theo, why didn't you push him down the stairs when you had the chance?'

The Nou Camp is magnificent. I had never seen it before, let alone played in it. I couldn't get over how steep the sides were. I felt a little bit worried for Mel because I knew she was going to be right in the top tier, and from down on the pitch it looked as though it would be the easiest thing to topple over the balcony on to the tier below. Watching from up there must be like peering down at a game from the window of an aeroplane.

The atmosphere inside the stadium on the night of the game was amazing, and we started well. Barcelona were full of confidence, but then we stunned them with a goal. Diaby played a great ball inside Maxwell for me to run on to and I was clean through on Victor Valdes, just like I had been at The Emirates. There had been no doubt in my mind about shooting then. This time was different. I thought I was going to shoot, but then, out of the corner of my eye, I saw Nicklas sprinting towards the box. I did what you're never supposed to do and got caught in two minds. Shall I shoot or give it to Nicklas? Most of the stuff I have done in my career I've done without thinking, but this time I was thinking hard. When that happens, you almost always make a mess of it. So what I did was give Nicklas a hospital pass. It was just behind him, so that instead of carrying on with his run he had to check back a little bit and allow his marker the chance of making a tackle. To his credit, Nicklas managed to turn it into a good ball and still got a shot in. Valdes saved it, but Nicklas rammed the rebound into the net. We were ahead. It was a glimpse of a fairy story.

A minute later we had the chance to do the same again. I was free down the right and Diaby could have played me in, but he either didn't see me or chose to ignore me and played the ball to the other flank. The chance was lost. Barcelona regained possession, went down the other end, and Messi scored a fantastic goal to put them level. We had been in the lead for two minutes.

If we had just been able to keep it tight for another few minutes and give them and their crowd the chance to get restless and nervy, who knows what would have happened. Instead, it turned into a Messi masterclass. It was like the ball was glued to his feet that night. For most people, it was the night that confirmed him as the best player in the world. He scored twice more before half-time, the second a lovely chip over Almunia, and rounded things off two minutes before the end. It was the best individual performance I've ever seen, and now that time has dulled the disappointment a little, I can even say I feel privileged to have been on the pitch when Messi scored four. I don't think anyone would have beaten Barcelona that night.

The Boss was calm afterwards. He said he was very proud of the way we had played at times and how we'd tried to get back into the match. But I felt they'd wanted it a bit more than us, especially in the second leg. They were sharper than us. They were like Arsenal on fast forward. It was an education playing against them. Inter Milan did a job on them in the semi-finals, but nothing will change my opinion that Barcelona are the best team in Europe.

There was a certain amount of acceptance about losing to Barcelona. We could rationalize the defeat because we recognized that we had come up against a superb team. It was a lot harder to deal with what happened when we rejoined the race for the Premier League title because by then many people had begun to tip us as unlikely champions, principally because we had such a favourable run-in.

We had gone top of the table briefly when we beat West Ham at The Emirates on 20 March, and even though a draw at Birmingham had moved us down to second, we were still right in the shake-up for the title when we got back from Barcelona and prepared to face Spurs in the north London derby at White Hart Lane eight days later. But we let everybody down that night. We fell behind to a wonder goal from their young left-back Danny Rose and we never really recovered.

I was on the bench again that night. The Boss picked Eboué ahead of me. I thought I'd been doing well coming off the bench in other games, and I'd laid on the goal for Nicklas in Barcelona. My own strategy would have been to play me from the start and try to win the game early, rather than trying to keep it tight for an hour and then bringing me on, but that wasn't the way the Boss was thinking of my role at that point in the season. I came on early in the second half at Spurs but I couldn't help turn things around. We lost 2–1, and it felt as though our chance of the title had slipped away.

But then, the following Saturday, Spurs beat Chelsea as well. John Terry was sent off and it seemed like Chelsea's challenge might be falling apart. Manchester United had beaten Manchester City with a late Paul Scholes goal, but it still seemed as though we might have been reprieved. We travelled up to the next match at Wigan Athletic thinking that all was not lost.

We played well in the first half. I started the match and opened the scoring with a neat finish four minutes before half-time. Mikael Silvestre put us further ahead just after the interval. We were cruising. We thought our title shot was back on track. Then we blew it. Wigan scored three goals in the last ten minutes and it was all over. There was no way back this time.

I have never seen the Boss more angry than he was after that game. He was furious. He had given us a heavy dressing down at half-time when we played Liverpool at Anfield before Christmas and had stunk the place out in the first forty-five minutes, but this was worse. He was throwing stuff and kicking other stuff, and there was a lot of swearing.

I didn't want to catch his eye. None of the players did. So we all had our heads down. I kept sneaking the odd glance just to keep a check on where he was. At one point he grabbed a load of sticks of chewing gum and was chucking them everywhere. I saw Pat Rice, his assistant, sit down while the Boss was swearing at the defence and having a go at them about how they had dropped off too much and allowed Wigan's forwards too much space. Then he whacked the seat next to Pat Rice and I saw Pat jump in shock.

Sol Campbell, who had been brought back to the club after his move to Notts County went bad, was having a go at everyone as well. He was saying, 'It's the Premier League, and no game's easy in the Premier League.' The Boss was walking back and forth quite a lot. It was probably the first time I'd seen him really lose it and it was scary.

He was right, of course. We should never have lost that game. We should have stayed in the title race until the bitter end. But we blew it with that defeat against Wigan. Chelsea and United moved out of our reach after that and we ended with a whimper, drawing with Manchester City, losing at Blackburn, and then finishing off by trouncing Fulham. But Fulham were in the Europa League Final in Hamburg the following Wednesday. They had a trophy to play for. We didn't.

It was a depressing end to a season that had begun holding out so much promise for the club. For a couple of months it had felt as though this might be the season when we really did shock everyone and when the Boss's faith in youth paid off. I got the impression that the neutrals would have loved us to win it, partly because of the shock value, partly because of our style of play, and partly because it would be a victory for the underdog against the might of Chelsea and United. But we couldn't deliver.

Every single year we talk about it being a young team, a team with potential, a team that will grow, but we can't use that excuse any more. We are experienced players now. We'd've put ourselves right back in there if we had won at Wigan, but we couldn't produce the performance when it mattered the most. Maybe we needed a bit of new blood. Everyone appreciates the Boss's loyalty to his players, but when we got money for Adebayor and Alexander Hleb we should have used it to replace them. If there was more competition, it would push us on even more.

I felt full of frustration at the end of 2009–10. It was a season to forget. For me it had been dominated by my injuries, but I also felt a lingering annoyance that whenever anything went wrong during a game and a change needed to be made, it was always take Theo off. It had happened less towards the end of the season, and I suppose, with the injuries I'd had, substituting me now and again made sense. But it starts to get into your head if you think you have to make an impression straight away or you're going to get hooked.

I wanted the Boss to have even more faith in me, but knew that would only come when I stayed injury-free and put a run of games together. As the season came to an end and thoughts turned to South Africa, I knew I had some catching up to do.

Twenty-two

On 2 April 2011 I was sitting in my room at the Four Seasons Hotel in Canary Wharf watching the game of football that I thought was about to decide Arsenal's season. Manchester United were 2–0 down to West Ham at Upton Park and it really seemed as though now we had Sir Alex Ferguson's side within reach and that at last we would be moving into prime position in the race for the title.

United started that game against West Ham, who were in the bottom three, on 63 points and we were on 58, with a game in hand. United's game in east London was a Saturday lunchtime kick-off and we were playing in the evening against Blackburn Rovers at The Emirates. It was the pivotal day of the season. Ferguson said that himself a few weeks later.

United were well on top in the first half. West Ham had only two attacks, but they scored from both of them. The United defence was caught out by a long ball for the first one, and when Carlton Cole lobbed it over Patrice Evra he batted it away with his hand and the referee gave a penalty. Mark Noble buried it, and when it hit the net I could feel my fist clenching. Noble scored a second penalty after twenty-five minutes, and Nemanja Vidic, who had looked especially shaky on the floor, was lucky to escape a red card in the minutes before half-time. If he had been sent off there would have been no way back for United.

I went down to the dining room for our pre-match meal feeling optimistic that United were going to lose. If they were defeated and we beat Blackburn, it would bring us to within two points of them and we would still have that game in hand. The other lads were buzzing at lunch. It seemed as though we were on the verge of being handed a great opportunity.

I should have known better. When I got back up to my room there were ten minutes left at Upton Park and United were winning. I soon gathered that Wayne Rooney had scored a hat-trick; I'd missed him swearing at the Sky camera. While I was watching, Javier Hernandez grabbed a fourth and the game was over. When I got on the coach with the rest of the lads to go to The Emirates, everyone looked deflated. The pressure was back on.

Ferguson admitted a few weeks later that the match had given his players a huge scare and the victory had spurred them on. It was the third time that season that they had come from two goals down to get something out of a game. Maybe that's what people mean when they say over and over again that Manchester United know what it takes to win a title. Maybe that's what experience brings you. Maybe if we had won titles before we would not have felt dispirited by what United had done. Maybe we too would have found the strength to carry on regardless and hunt them down.

We knew we had to match their result by beating Blackburn and restoring some momentum to our season. It seemed like we often played after United in that stretch, that we were always having to respond to them rather than the other way around. And against Blackburn, that pressure got to us.

Blackburn were in the middle of a run of eleven games without a win and sinking fast, and we really should have beaten them. But we were starting to tie up a little bit too, and we could not break them down. I forced a decent save out of Paul Robinson early in the first half and he frustrated us time and time again. Like a lot of sides at The Emirates,

Blackburn parked the bus and we just could not find a way through.

The fans got more and more irritated, and to be honest, so did the players. We knew that we had to win to keep United in our sights. We were aware of the importance of getting all three points, but even after they had Steven Nzonzi sent off for a shocking two-footed tackle on Laurent Koscielny, we could not break the deadlock. The game finished goalless. The fans were restless and disappointed. The opportunity had gone.

Now we were seven points behind United and our game in hand would not take us above them if we won it; a victory would just be helping us to play catch-up. The scenarios I had been mapping out in my mind while I was sitting in my room at the Four Seasons a few hours earlier were suddenly meaningless. And the dreadful weight of the prospect of another season without a trophy began to bear down on us.

That draw with Blackburn was actually the end of a desperate few weeks for us. Many said they felt that the turning point in our season was not 2 April but defeat to Birmingham City in the Carling Cup Final at Wembley on 27 February. A lot of people tend to mock the Carling Cup as a competition but it still holds plenty of significance in the English game, partly because of the timing of the final. Also, for a club like ours that had not won anything for some time, lifting a trophy – any trophy – had become incredibly important for our morale. The final comes at a stage in the season that effectively marks the beginning of the title run-in, the point when things are getting serious in the Champions League and the FA Cup too. The Carling Cup may not be as important as these competitions but it has the power to give you a real boost for the last couple of months of a campaign.

José Mourinho understood this when he was manager of Chelsea. The Carling Cup was the first trophy the club won when he was in charge. They went on to win the first of their back-to-back league titles under him that year. The Boss understood it, too. He knew that the Carling Cup was the least of our targets in 2010–11 but that winning it could be a stepping stone to the bigger prizes.

Going into the Carling Cup Final, I thought we were going to win the Premier League title. I really believed that. I thought we had the confidence and I thought we had the players. But we seem to have an unfortunate knack of picking up injuries at really bad times, and it happened again.

I didn't play at Wembley. Both Cesc Fabregas and I were injured in the midweek match against Stoke the previous Wednesday. I got an ankle sprain that put me out for a month so I was a spectator for the final. It wasn't easy sitting in the stands. We went a goal behind from a set-piece when Nikola Zigic rose above our defence to head the ball past Wojciech Szczesny, but when Robin Van Persie equalized before half-time I thought we were there. If we had won that final, we would have wanted more and more. We would have got the taste for it again.

The fact that the Birmingham keeper, Ben Foster, was named man-of-the-match after the game showed that we were the better team and that we had more chances, but I never felt comfortable and two minutes from the end we self-destructed. Zigic again won a header, on the edge of the box, and as Koscielny went to clear it Szczesny came to collect it and they got in each other's way. The ball squirmed away from Szczesny and straight into the path of Obafemi Martins, who had come on as a substitute five minutes earlier. He couldn't miss. He knocked the ball into the open goal and the trophy was Birmingham's.

It was the worst possible way for us to lose and it knocked the stuffing out of us. We were slaughtered in the media the next day and all the old uncomfortable questions about our goalkeeping situation, our defence and our mental strength came flooding out into the open again. At the worst possible time in our season, our morale plummeted. That defeat, in a tournament that used to be known as the Worthless Cup, killed us.

Our season fell apart after that. In our next league game, at The Emirates, we slid to a goalless draw with Sunderland and then lost 3–1 to Barcelona at the Nou Camp in the second leg of our Champions League second-round tie after Robin was sent off in bizarre circumstances early in the second half.

The first leg, ten days before the Carling Cup Final, had been special. I'm not being wide-eyed about it, but to start a game like that and be on the same pitch as Lionel Messi was a thrill. Those are the occasions you play the game for, competing against the best and testing yourself against the best. And I think everyone realizes that at the moment Barcelona are about as good as it gets.

They were superb at The Emirates. Just like they had been the season before. But we were closer to them this time. We were doing a lot of chasing but we counter-attacked very well and in the second half we began to cause them problems. They had gone 1–0 up through a clinical finish by David Villa mid-way through the first half and even though they dominated possession, we never gave up. I came off thirteen minutes from the end, and a minute after that

Robin equalized with a fierce shot that beat Victor Valdes at his near post. Five minutes after that, Nasri crossed for Arshavin who arrived late on the edge of the box and curled a shot first time past the goal-keeper for the winner.

It was a special achievement. Not many sides beat Barcelona, home or away. In many ways they had been the better side, but we won the game. We found a way to win. When Manchester United were out-classed by Messi and the rest in the Champions League Final a few months later, it brought it home to a lot of people exactly what we had done at The Emirates that evening.

That match was notable for something else, too: Jack Wilshere played like a dream in the centre of our midfield and attracted rave reviews afterwards. Jack was always going to have a fine career at Arsenal. His loan spell at Bolton at the end of the previous season had accelerated his development and right from the start of 2010–11 it was clear he was going to be a big part of our team. He looked totally at home against Barcelona. His technique stood up to the intense press-ing Barcelona subjected us to and he always seemed to have time on the ball, in the same way that Xavi and Andres Iniesta do. After the game, several writers said he had been so impressive it was more likely that Barcelona would try to buy Jack than Cesc.

But by the time the second leg came around our momentum had gone. I was still out injured after the ankle sprain against Stoke and Cesc was not fully fit. For the neutral, for people who love football, Barcelona were a joy to watch again that night in the Nou Camp and they deserved to go ahead on the stroke of half-time, even if the nature of their goal was difficult for us to take.

Cesc received the ball on the edge of our box and tried a risky move by backheeling it towards Jack. It went to Iniesta instead, and he played a beautiful pass through to Messi. As Almunia came out to meet him, Messi dinked the ball over him and then volleyed the ball into the net. It was a sublime piece of skill, but Cesc was furious with himself for the initial mistake.

I was watching at home in Hertfordshire. I thought the game was over then, but ten minutes after half-time we got a rare corner and Sergio Busquets headed into his own goal. We were back ahead on aggregate.

Three minutes later the tie turned back in Barcelona's favour. Robin ran on to a through-ball, took a touch and then shot wide, but he had not heard the referee blow for offside. The referee decided he had been time-wasting and showed him a second yellow card, then a red. It was an unbelievably harsh decision, a terrible decision. No one could quite believe it. There were a couple of seconds between the referee blowing his whistle and Robin taking his shot. And it was hard enough playing Barcelona with eleven men, let alone ten. The Spanish side cut loose from that moment on. Xavi and Messi scored in quick succession and we were hanging on for dear life.

But we were still only one goal away from qualifying. And in the dying minutes Jack broke away through the middle and slid a perfect ball through for Nicklas Bendtner, who had just come on for Cesc, to go one-on-one with Valdes. I leapt off the sofa in my lounge, ready to run around the room when he stuck it in because that would have put us through on away goals. You need to take chances like that at the top level, but Bendtner's first touch was poor and it allowed Valdes to make a block. It was our last opportunity.

We could complain all we wanted about the significance of Robin's sending-off but nursing a grievance wasn't going to change anything. We were out of the competition. The following weekend we went out of the FA Cup too, beaten 2–0 at Old Trafford by United. Then we drew at West Brom in the league. So when, the weekend after that, United came from behind to win at West Ham and we dropped another two points in that scoreless draw against Blackburn, it felt as if our season was over.

We still had tantalizing chances to get back into the title race but our failure to take them became like a kind of slow torture. On 17 April we took a 1–0 lead against Liverpool at The Emirates in the ninety-eighth minute with a penalty and then gave away another penalty four minutes later when Eboué had a rush of blood to the head and barged into Lucas. Dirk Kuyt buried the spot-kick. So we were six points behind United with six to play.

The next Wednesday we went to Spurs with a glimmer of hope because United had drawn at Newcastle the previous evening. We couldn't have started any better. I ran on to a through-ball from Cesc after five minutes and tucked it past Heurelho Gomes into the bottom corner.

I loved scoring that goal, partly because of the importance of the occasion and partly because it reinforced my belief that I can play through the middle more and more in the years ahead. I'm convinced now that that's my best position and I hope I can start to persuade the Boss of that. I think he feels the same, but it's a question of how I fit in with Robin and whether there is a replacement for me on the right.

Most of my goals have come from runs made coming inside from the right. That goal against Spurs, those are the sorts of runs I have watched Thierry Henry, Michael Owen and Freddie Ljungberg make on DVD. They are the three main people I watch and study. I have always watched Owen and Thierry. And recently I have watched DVDs of Freddie's runs with the aid of ProZone. Even if they didn't always end in goals, Freddie was a great maker of runs.

I want to play more up front but I certainly don't see it as a case of either me or Robin starting there. He's very important to my game. Sometimes at meetings he will say things like 'when Theo plays, I am a better player', and that is an incredible compliment coming from a player with his talent. It makes me want to set him up with more goals. We might have had our moments in the past but we get on incredibly well now.

After I'd put us ahead at White Hart Lane, Rafael Van Der Vaart equalized two minutes later. We took a 3–1 lead but let it slip. It was a great match but it wasn't much consolation when it finished 3–3. We had let another two points go begging. We were still six behind United and now Chelsea had overtaken us to move into second place as well.

We lost to Bolton on 24 April, so when we beat United at The Emirates seven days later, it was too late. In fact, that victory only added to our sense of frustration at the way we had let things go. We went on to lose at Stoke and then again at home to Aston Villa. After contending for the title for so long in what had been a two-horse race we ended up fourth as Manchester City nosed past us too.

It was all a dreadful anti-climax. And of course there was a sense of déjà vu. We had fallen away just like that the previous season. We had a couple of freak results, like the 4–4 draw at Newcastle at the beginning of February when we blew a 4–0 lead, but our home form let us down too. We lost to West Brom, Newcastle, Spurs and Aston Villa at The Emirates. United didn't lose a single game at Old Trafford.

I don't know how to explain our home form, really. There is a lot of pressure at The Emirates and the fans have been quite quick to get on our backs. I totally understand that because they pay their money and we have not been good enough, but a lot of teams park the bus at The Emirates and we find it difficult to break them down.

There were times, too, when it felt we would have to score three to win a game because we had not been strong enough defensively as a unit. People talked a lot about our failure to sign a goalkeeper in the summer of 2010 but I think the manager's faith in Wojciech will pay off from here on in. I've always liked him as a keeper. He has got a lot of stature and I think he's good enough. I think he'll be number one for some time. He is starting to become more assertive and if the players start to think he's a prick on the pitch, that's fine. Jens Lehmann was the nicest guy off the pitch, but on the pitch he was a pain in the arse.

I took some consolation from my own development. The highlights of my season were my goals and assists, nine and seven respectively in the Premier League, and that was in a season when I missed thirteen weeks through injury. I can do better but I'm moving in the right direction. I've worked really hard on my final ball. I always stick around after training and practise shooting and crossing with the mannequins, trying to make sure I get my crosses past the first man.

Sometimes, with the way we play, it's difficult to pick out people with crosses, because we tend not to pack the box. Ironically, the best cross I did last season was nicked off Robin's head by the hand of Nemanja Vidic in the game against United at The Emirates. The linesman didn't see it, Vidic got away with it. If the referee had seen it Vidic would have been sent off and would have missed a crucial match against Chelsea, which United won. Another 'what if'.

I had to hold on to things like that to cope with the disappointment of the way our season petered out. It was a strange ride. Halfway through it I even admitted to diving during our FA Cup third-round tie against Leeds United. I felt a weak tug on my shirt from Paul Connolly and I went down. The referee, Phil Dowd, awarded a penalty initially and then changed his mind.

I don't know why I felt guilty about it, really. Technically, there was an infringement, but I felt that I could have stayed on my feet. I have always thought of myself as an honest player and I didn't like to think that I had done anything that could be construed as gamesmanship so I went in front of the television cameras and apologized for my actions.

Nobody seemed to know whether to praise me or condemn me. I was beginning to get used to that. After what had happened before the World Cup the previous summer, I could cope.

Twenty-three

I was desperate to go to the 2010 World Cup finals. I felt it would complete a cycle for me. I had gone to Germany in 2006 but in many ways that summer I was The Man Who Wasn't There. I was a ghost, someone who was included in the squad but who was somehow still an outsider. As I've said, I wasn't really ready then, but as the tournament in South Africa approached I got more and more excited about it, confident that I could make a big contribution.

The build-up was troubled. Mr Capello had stripped John Terry of the England captaincy at the beginning of February following allegations surrounding his personal life. It didn't have any impact on me. It felt like JT was always the captain anyway, even though he didn't have the armband on. Everyone still looked at him like he was the captain, and I didn't think he should have lost it. JT would die for England. He would do anything for the team on the pitch. And that should have been all that mattered. But the situation was complicated by the involvement of Wayne Bridge, and Mr Capello had a difficult decision to make. From around that time, though, our form began to slide. Having been so impressive in the qualifying tournament, we lost a bit of momentum. Our players began to tire as the 2009–10 season wore on and we began to struggle a little bit.

I was fighting injury all the time so I was in and out of the England side. I didn't feel out of place when I joined up any more but there was something very stiff and starchy about Mr Capello's regime before the World Cup. I found it difficult to be myself. Players split up along club lines. There was an Aston Villa group and a Manchester United group and the staff weren't very relaxed. It all felt a bit tense. Everyone was a bit too serious.

One of the best mixers, one of the people who moved easily between the different cliques, was Wayne Rooney. He's such an easy bloke to get along with and he's popular with everybody. In the future, I think he'll make a great England captain. He's got a talent for bringing people together and he's got the kind of charisma that will make people want to follow him as a leader.

By the spring I was starting to get a bit worried about my place in the World Cup squad because I had been out for so long with injuries. I was thinking I had to start playing to have a chance of going to South Africa. I needed to get back into the Arsenal team.

It is usually easy to come into a winning team, but when I did come back I was putting too much pressure on myself. I wanted to be back to my best straight away, but you need six or seven games to get back into the swing of things, back into the routine. I knew that Aaron Lennon was in a rich vein of form for Spurs and everyone was rightly praising him for that and saying he was a certainty to be in the national squad. That kind of thing stays in the back of your mind. I was looking around at my rivals who all seemed to be fighting fit and in top form and wishing someone would have a few bad games. I feel awful about that but I'm sure all players think the same. Everyone wants to play. It's human nature.

The constant speculation about whether I would recover properly for the World Cup started to cause tension with Arsenal, too. At press conferences before Arsenal games, Mr Wenger was still being asked about my chances of making Capello's squad. I think the Boss realized the situation was worrying me a bit, too, though. He knew how desperate I was to go to

South Africa. He pulled me once and told me that Franco Baldini, Mr Capello's right-hand man, had told him I was guaranteed to go to the World Cup if I was fit. That reassured me a lot.

I started the friendly against Egypt at Wembley at the beginning of March. I had a decent run early on, got to the byline and pulled a cross back into the path of Frank Lampard. His shot went over the bar, and then midway through the half Egypt took the lead. We were a bit flat and I think I was probably trying a bit too hard. People expect me to beat five or six players all the time, and that isn't going to happen.

We equalized early in the second half, and a minute later Mr Capello took me off and replaced me with Shaun Wright-Phillips. Shaun played superbly. He scored one and set one up for Peter Crouch. I was sitting on the bench, part pleased for him, part thinking, 'Shit!' and wishing that Lamps had buried his earlier chance, which might have cast my performance in a different light.

I didn't have a great game but I wasn't too bad. Still, it didn't stop me being slaughtered after the match. Now I don't mind criticism if it is constructive, because you learn from that, but this was different. As a rule, the people I listen to are my managers, coaches and teammates.

Anyway, when Mr Capello named his thirty-man provisional World Cup squad on 11 May, I was in it. There was no surprise about my inclusion. I had finally played a run of games for Arsenal and had shown some decent form. I had put the injuries behind me at just the right time and I felt fresh and ready to go. I knew there was plenty of competition from people like Aaron, Shaun, Adam Johnson, James Milner and Joe Cole but I knew that Mr Baldini had told the Boss I would go if I was fit, so I was still confident about my place.

There were two warm-up games against Mexico and Japan arranged before we left for South Africa, but before those we headed out to a training camp in the Austrian Alps, a couple of hours' bus journey from Graz. We stayed at the Hotel Schloss Pichlarn, a grand 1,000-year-old castle that carried slightly uncomfortable echoes of the Schlosshotel Bühlerhöhe where we stayed in Baden-Baden during the 2006 World Cup. Mr Capello had used the venue for pre-season training when he was manager of Real Madrid and it offered the added benefit of preparing us for playing at altitude in South Africa. We trained on a pitch that was open to the public on one side, which was a bit of a bonus for the journalists who travelled out from England. They mingled with the locals but we could spot some of them a mile off.

Something happened out there that shook my confidence. It was the second day, and I made a run inside from my position out wide on the right. Suddenly, Mr Capello started screaming at me at the top of his voice. Training stopped and everyone stared at their feet and looked embarrassed. 'Theo,' he was yelling, 'I will kill you if you come inside like that again!'

I couldn't believe it. I was happy to obey instructions and stay out wide. I knew that was what he wanted from me. But now and again I was going to drift inside. Otherwise it's too predictable. But he was making it very clear he wanted me rigidly out wide. So I hugged the touchline and I hardly touched the ball in training.

It made me feel inhibited and unsure. I felt I was on the point of getting back to the level I should have been at and I was really looking forward to the tournament, but that episode really shook me up. Despite Mr Capello's outburst, I never quite knew what was required of me. I was confused. They were telling me to get more involved one minute then telling me to hug the touchline the next.

I just felt like there wasn't much help coming from the staff. There was no one to put an arm round you. I had been injured so much that season that my confidence was fragile, but no one ever helped me. It was difficult to go up to someone and talk to them. I thought maybe Stuart Pearce could have said something, but there was nothing.

The rest of the lads wound me up about it afterwards and we had a laugh, but inside it hurt me a bit. I'd had a difficult season and I needed my confidence building up. If you are the boss, surely you want everyone playing well and you want to encourage everyone. That was only the second day in. It killed me, and I felt it wasn't fair. Maybe Mr Capello wanted more out of me, but he would have got more out of me if I had been allowed to come inside as well.

We flew back to London to play Mexico at Wembley. I started, and I did OK. It was a warm-up match and it was another average performance but I played for all but the last thirteen minutes and we won 3–1. Then we flew back to Austria to get ready for the Japan friendly in Graz.

I struggled in that match, no question, but I was hardly alone in that. We were outplayed by Japan in the first half and Mr Capello brought five of us off at the interval, including me. One of the substitutes, Joe Cole, put in a man-of-the-match performance in the second half and turned the game. We won 2–1, courtesy of two Japan own goals.

We flew back to England after the match. It was a

Sunday. Mr Capello was due to name his final twenty-three-man squad on the Tuesday. The guessing games about who would be in and who would be left at home began in earnest. Most of the speculation surrounded whether Gareth Barry would be named because of an ankle injury he had sustained late in the season, or whether Owen Hargreaves would grab the place instead. It was generally thought the final choice was between taking a specialist reserve left-back, Stephen Warnock, or Shaun Wright-Phillips.

I felt 100 per cent sure I would be going. Not just because I had already had my picture taken in my official England World Cup suit, but because of what Franco Baldini had told the Boss, and because I had confidence in myself that I could make an impact in South Africa. At the very least, I thought I had shown that season against Barcelona, the best club team in the world, that I could come off the bench and hurt a side. I knew that my build-up could have been better, but I was coming back to form after a long season struggling with injury.

You want to know how sure I was that I was going? Well, I'd packed my bag, put it that way.

On the day the squad was announced, I went to Brocket Hall near my home in Hertfordshire for a last round of golf before leaving for South Africa. I was out on the course with my cousin, Nick, and my mate from the youth team at Southampton, Jake Thomson. I was standing on the fairway on the fourth hole when my mobile phone rang and I saw Mr Capello's name on the screen.

I answered it. The reception was terrible and I could only just hear Mr Capello's voice. I couldn't really make out what he was saying but I thought I heard the word 'sorry'. Then the line went dead.

My heart started beating really fast. I still didn't really believe I wouldn't be going. I thought maybe he was saying sorry that the line was bad. I called him back, and this time the line was clear.

He was short and to the point. He said he was sorry but I hadn't made the squad and I wouldn't be going to the World Cup. I wanted to ask him why, but I didn't get the chance. He said I would be a big part of his plans for the European Championship in 2012, and that was it, really. I tried to say something else but the line just went dead again. It was over.

I was stunned. It would be dishonest to say otherwise. I had a bit of a cry and Jake and Nick tried to console me. I had wanted so much to go to South Africa. It had assumed massive importance for me. It was the last thing I needed to do to wipe out the disappointment of not getting a kick in Germany four years earlier, and now the chance to do it had been snatched away. I couldn't believe it.

I finished the round of golf. I thought I might as well. It postponed the inevitability of facing up to the news and the sympathy. I played the best golf I've ever played. It must have been the anger. I respected Mr Capello's decision, but I went through a whole mix of emotions in just a few days – I was numb, shocked, upset, angry, confused. I realized I had to look at myself as well. I blamed myself, and I still do. I had tried to regain my fitness after the injuries but the football just wasn't happening. When you only play bit parts in games, it's difficult to get back into a proper rhythm.

Aaron Lennon and Shaun Wright-Phillips both made the squad. So did Joe Cole. And Stephen Warnock got in even though he hadn't played a single minute in those two warm-up games. Gareth Barry was in, too. I was absolutely distraught not to be going. I wasn't alone. Michael Dawson, Leighton Baines, Adam Johnson, Tom Huddlestone, Scott Parker and Darren Bent were the others to miss out on the final party.

The media seemed almost as startled as me when the news broke. The front page of the *Sun* the next day had a picture of me in my England suit under the headline 'Suited and Booted'. Some commentators said I had only myself to blame and that Mr Capello had made a brave and correct decision; others said

that he had missed an opportunity to include someone who at the very least could have made a big
impact coming off the bench.

I didn't escape on holiday straight away. I thought
I ought to stay professional about it and stick around
in case someone had to drop out through injury. I was
still clinging to a shred of hope. It wasn't that I
was praying for Aaron or Shaun or Joe to get injured.
They're all human beings with the same hopes as me
and the same desire to prove themselves, and we are
all teammates. But that does not stop you hoping you
might get some sort of reprieve. But the reprieve
never came. Michael Dawson was called up when Rio
Ferdinand was injured on the eve of the tournament,
but that was it.

I went on holiday to Las Vegas and watched the
USA game over breakfast in the restaurant at
the Palazzo. We were up off our seats when Stevie G
put us ahead and then we were deafened by the
cheers and the guffaws when poor Rob Green made
the error that allowed the USA to equalize.

There are lots of conflicting emotions going on
when you have been left out of an event like that and
you are forced to watch from the sidelines. I don't
know what I would have done if we had won the
tournament. Part of me would have been ecstatic but
part of me would have been destroyed for missing out

on it. I have heard about the effect that being left out of England's World Cup Final side had on Jimmy Greaves. I don't like to contemplate what he must have gone through.

I didn't see the Algeria game because I was on a trip to the Grand Canyon. From what I've heard, that was a mercy. And by the time we played Germany in the last sixteen I had gone to Crete with Mel. I didn't see that game either. I was on a boat so it was the skipper who told me we'd been knocked out. I was desperately sorry for the boys, particularly when I found out about the injustice that had been done to them over Frank Lampard's goal that never was. But a small part of me was glad that the torture of my exclusion from the squad was over and I could now try to get on with the rest of my career.

Things have gone well since then. I came straight back into the first team after the World Cup and have been selected for Euro 2012 qualifiers when I've been fit. Around the turn of the year, Mr Capello said that the one regret he had about his World Cup squad selection was that he didn't take me. He said it had been a mistake to leave me out. It was big of him to admit that because he didn't need to, and it meant a lot to me.

The atmosphere with England is much more relaxed now. There are more smiles around the England camp these days. Mr Capello has changed;

lots of things have changed. He is more approachable. I played in the first game after the World Cup, a friendly at home to Hungary, and at training the day before the match I walked up to him on the sideline and asked him why I hadn't gone to South Africa. He just said he didn't think I was ready. He said he thought that the World Cup had come a little bit too early for me.

That's two World Cups that have come too early for me then. Playing at the Greatest Show on Earth is still an itch I need to scratch. It's one of a few more chapters I need to write.

Index

Theo Walcott was born on 16 March 1989 and grew up near Newbury in Berkshire. After joining the youth scheme at Southampton, he became the Saints' youngest ever player, before moving to Arsenal in a £12m transfer in January 2006.

Following his surprise selection in Sven-Göran Eriksson's World Cup squad, Theo set another record in making his England debut at the age of just 17 years and 75 days, and was named the BBC's Young Sports Personality of the Year in 2006.

He is now a star forward for both Arsenal and England and in September 2008 became the youngest player in history to score a hat-trick for England.